If you are in Tbilisi you are welcome at TBC Bank

TBILISI

A GUIDE

John FR Wright

To Lilian and Olga

© W&M Press, 4 Tatishvili Lane, Tbilisi, Georgia. Email: wandmpress@access.sanet.ge

I.S.B.N. 99928-0-069-0

Typeset & Design: W&M Press and Calamus Graphics

Photography: Natalia Mordovina

Cover illustration: *Akhvlediani Rise*

Grateful thanks to: Suren Gevinyan, Irma and Eka Khvedelidze, Maia Mania, Peter Nasmyth, David Sakhveralidze and David Sulakvelidze.

Printed and bound in Georgia by: Calamus Graphics Studio, Tbilisi.

Orders, Updates and Information: www.tbilisigeorgia.com

Cataloguing in Publication Data: *A catalogue record is available from the Georgian National Library*

CONTENTS

View of the Old Town from
Baratashvili Bridge

INTRODUCTION

Tbilisi is a city rich in both art and history. Throughout its long and turbulent past the city has been a meeting point for different peoples and cultures. Founded as the nation's capital in the fifth century, Tbilisi winds along the contours made from the valley of the Mtkvari River. Nestled between the Sololaki Range of mountains to the south, Mount Makhata to the east and the foothills of the Trialeti Range to the west, the city appears as a natural place for settlement. On clear spring and autumnal days, the highest peaks of the Caucasus Mountains are visible from the city centre.

Home today to nearly one and half million people, the city continues its long cosmopolitan tradition. During mediaeval times, Arabs, Armenians, Azeris, Kurds, Persians, Turks and later Russians would venture and settle in Tbilisi together with the indigenous Georgians. Today Americans, West Europeans and others are adding to the city's colour.

The country's recent independence has set the capital at the apex of important and strategic plans for revitalising trading routes of yore and forging new associations in the modern world.

Best visited in spring and autumn, the climate of Tbilisi is temperate with hot summers and mild winters. January and February are the coldest months with average temperatures between zero to five degrees celsius. July and August are the hottest months when temperatures often exceed thirty degrees celsius. March and April witness the transition from winter towards summer and are often characterised by strong winds and sudden showers. May and June are delightful months as are September and October.

Looking towards
Narikala

9

As the city takes on a new life as the proud head of an independent nation, so the need for a volume that describes Tbilisi's essential character and particular features. This is what this guide intends to do. It is separated into what are hopefully useful sections and is designed both for the short-term visitor as well as someone who may be coming to live and work for a longer period. The routes indicated for exploring the city are no more than suggestions but provide perhaps the best way to see the major treasures Tbilisi has to offer. Included are a number of photographs of the major historical buildings and monuments of the town in the hope that this volume may also be a suitable memento of one's time in the city.

Additionally there are listings to accommodation facilities, as well as to the best restaurants and bars. In both cases the number and quality of hotels and restaurants is increasing. Anyone visiting Tbilisi will want to try Georgian cuisine and included in this guide is an explanation of the main national dishes.

The section on practicalities hopefully will make your visit easier and more enjoyable. Plunging into a new culture with its particular ways of life and one that has its own unique language and script can be a little daunting. Included are suggestions on shopping and how to use the city's excellent public transport system. Additionally there are two maps covering the Old Town and the City Centre.

It is little secret that over the past ten to fifteen years the struggle for independence, the ensuing civil strife and the process of converting the country as a whole to a more market economy has wrought considerable toil to the fabric of the city. As you wander the streets of the city, particularly in the old town you will notice that some quarters are crumbling and are in need of renovation and restoration. To help alleviate some of the problems a successful application has been made to UNESCO to include historical Tbilisi in the list of protected monuments of the world. Moreover a civic organization has been established to seek ways of preserving and renewing the capital.

Nevertheless through the winding streets of the old town to the nineteenth and twentieth century centre of the city and onto the modern suburbs, at every turn there is something interesting to see and experience. Tbilisi was for many years a secret as it was almost completely hidden away from the view of the world. Thankfully today anyone can visit and are more than welcome. Tbilisians you will find are some of the most hospitable people imaginable.

Welcome to Tbilisi!

ORIGINS

Archaeologists attest to some form of human habitation as long ago as five thousand years before Christ. The Caucasus region as a whole would appear to be one of the very earliest geographical regions of human existence. In this sense the Caucasus has become one of the 'cradles of civilisation'. Burial grounds and dwellings have been found in and around the old town straddling the Mtkvari riverbed dating from the Neolithic period. However it was not until much later in the fifth century that Tbilisi grew to prominence and became the capital of an emerging Georgian state. From the third century BC until the fifth century AD, Mtskheta, some twenty kilometres to the north west of Tbilisi, had been the capital of the country. As with most origins there is a tale of how Tbilisi came to be the chosen place.

A certain King Vakhtang was out hunting one day from his palace in Mtskheta. He spied a pheasant in the undergrowth and aiming his arrow shot the bird. The pheasant fell into a spring and as Vakhtang went to recover his prey, he found it revitalised. He was so impressed by the water healing properties of the spring that he immediately decided upon relocating his capital to this site.

King Vakhtang Gorgasali

11

The tale may have some resonance in fact. There was a king called Vakhtang Gorgasali (447-502) who ruled Eastern Georgia or as it was then known Iberia. The word Iberia appears to derive from Greek, meaning the place 'out there'. Both the ancient Greeks and Romans had for periods controlled parts of Georgia. By the fifth century and one hundred years after the adoption of Christianity in 337, Western Georgia or as it was called Colchis was under the control of Byzantium, while in Iberia to the east King Vakhtang was at least at the start of his rule in alliance with Iran. The division of the country into spheres of influence by foreign powers is a common theme throughout the country's history. Local rulers like Vakhtang constantly battled for autonomy and a greater say in their own affairs by trying to placate outsiders and by shifting allegiance when circumstances were propitious for doing so. Thus in 482 Vakhtang changed his orientation and joined Byzantium against Sassanid Iran. Three years of war ensued. Vakhtang sealed his new alliance by marriage to Helena, the daughter of Emperor Zeno and remained loyal to Byzantium for the rest of his life even though he spent much of it at war or in exile. Quite when therefore, the decision to move from Mtskheta to Tbilisi was made, remains something of a mystery. It may have been that once free of Iranian control Vakhtang, being impressed by the Narikala Fortress built by the Persians in the fourth century, took control of it for a period and declared the settlement surrounding it his capital as a consequence.

MEDIAEVAL PERIOD (500-1100)

Upon Vakhtang's death his heir, Dachi set about building the capital according to his father's plans. However Tbilisi was soon to fall under foreign dominion. Initially Vakhtang's descendants maintained a close association with Roman Byzantium. By doing so the emergent Georgian Church was strengthened and institutionalised. A number of churches were built during the period including the Anchiskhati church in Tbilisi that dates from the early sixth century. The continuing battle for dominion between Iran and Byzantium over the lands of the Caucasus resulted in a peace agreement in 591. Mtskheta and the lands to the west stretching to the Black Sea coast were deemed under Byzantine suzerainty, while Tbilisi and the regions of the east to the Caspian were Iranian. Iran was assisted by the local ruler of the period Stepanoz 1 (590-627). For while the overlords had reached some peaceful accommodation about the apportioning of influence over the territories, Stepanoz 1 believed he might use the fact that Byzantine was involved in a struggle with the North Caucasian Avars to gain more power for himself. He switched allegiance from Rome to Persia and marched from Mtskheta and took the Narikala Fortress above the Mtkvari River.

He had however seriously miscalculated. For galvanised by victory over the Avar hordes, the new Byzantine emperor Heraclius 1 (610-614) launched campaigns into the heartland of Iberia, cap-

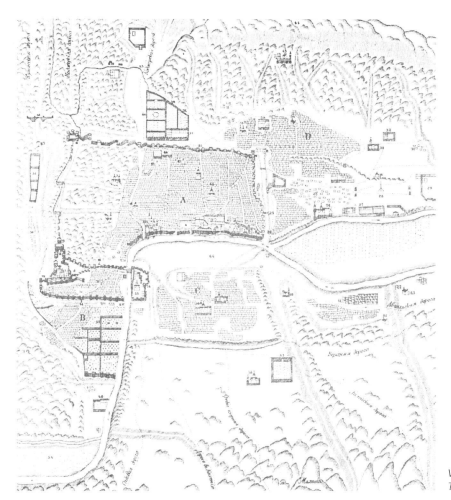

Vakhushti's Map of Tbilisi 1735

tured Tbilisi and as the Georgian Chronicles put it, flailed Stepanoz alive. Byzantium maintained effective control over Iberia until the arrival of a new force in Caucasian life, the Arabs. Spreading forth from their base in the Arabian heartland and already with Egypt, Syria and the Levant under their sway, the Arabs moved north. Sassanid Iran was now a weakened state and Byzantium was at full tilt restricting the advancing Arab charge in other parts of Asia Minor. Arriving through Armenia that was captured in 640, the Arabs took Tbilisi in 645 and remained in charge until the period of Georgia's golden age some four hundred or so years later.

Undoubtedly the character of the city changed with the new overlords. Due to the later sackings of the city, there are no architectural remains of the Arab period, and for a sense of life and the struggle of Georgia's Christianity for survival against the Islamic onslaught we must turn to the stories of the saints of the country. One such was a certain Martyr Abo of Tbilisi.

Martyr Abo as his name suggests was an Arab by birth. A native of Baghdad and maker of aromatic ointments at the age of seventeen he moved to Tbilisi. Abo soon learned the Georgian language and studied the Scriptures. A convert to Christianity he proved a thorn in the side of the Caliph overlords. The Arabs realised that there was little hope of converting the Georgian peasants in the countryside but were fearful of Christian followers peddling their influence in the cities. Abo was steeped in Christian asceticism and piety. As the chroniclers relate 'the Saint was confined in a dungeon and then brought to trial'. By persuasion and promises of all minds of wealth and honours, they attempted to return him to Islam. Despite repeated whippings and lashings to his body Abo remained unwavering in his faith. He was executed on 6 January 786. Oil was poured over his body and set alight on the cliff above the river – the very spot today where the Metechi church stands. But according to the tale, God sent a star that shone like a lamp, and illuminated the whole of Tbilisi long into the night. On the next day, his executioners threw his charred bones down into the river below but immediately an amazing pillar of light was thrown up from the water.

Arab rule dissipated during the tenth century, particularly in eastern Georgia or what was now called Kartli. Meanwhile the Byzantium Empire was expanding. Under Basil II (972-1025), Byzantium extended its lands eastward. This proved a turning point for Tbilisi and Georgia as a whole. The local rulers of the period, in alliance with Emperor Basil, managed to liberate lands both in the west of the country and the east and as the eleventh century dawned a new word was coined representing the land of Georgia. For under Bagrat III (975-1014), Sakartvelo or the land where the Georgians (Kartvelians) are, became a unified entity and for the first time with Tbilisi as its central capital. This unity was short-lived. Seljuk Turks in control of Iran moved eastwards during the eleventh century. Tbilisi fell along with swathes of Georgian land. Georgians refer to this period as the wars of the *Didi Turkoba*. The country fragmented once again and royal power was severely weakened. Tbilisi was left in the hands of its own citizens who ruled it more or less independently.

GOLDEN AGE (1100-1300)

Tbilisi regained its Georgian and Christian roots during the reign of David Aghmashenebeli (The Builder) (1089-1125). King David first set about attacking the Seljuk Turks in the periphery of

*David Aghmashenebeli
(The Builder)*

Georgia and with success. His timing was propitious as this was the period of the crusades from Western Europe into the Holy Land. Buoyed by his victories, David refused to pay tributes to the Turks, and encouraged the indigenous Georgians to return to their homes from their mountain refuges. Moreover he speedily dealt with potential rival local kings and princes and purged the Georgian ecclesiastical orders. With the rural areas of the country under his control and having centralised much of the apparatus of a state, only Tbilisi and the cities of Dmanisi and Ganja lay outside his control. The inhabitants of these cities looked to the Seljuks for support to ward off David's seeming inevitable march upon them. Sultan Mahmud of Iraq gathered enormous funds for a campaign against King David. On August 12th 1121 David with Armenian, Kipchak, Ossetian and Shirvan allies attacked at a place not far from Tbilisi called Didgori. The resulting victory is known and celebrated by Georgians as *dzleva sakvirveli* (the wonderful victory).

In 1122 Tbilisi was taken. King David continued his battles and by his death in 1125 Tbilisi stood at the head of a multinational empire stretching from the Black Sea in the west and the Caspian Sea in the east. His successors built upon the military success and established a generally peaceful and stable state. Following a brief flirtation with disaster as David's immediate successors fought with each other for control, Giorgi III in 1177 had the foresight to crown his daughter co-ruler of Georgia and signal clearly his chosen successor. Under Queen Tamar (1184-1213), Georgia and Tbilisi blossomed.

Such is the veneration that Tamar was held and indeed still is that she is often referred to as King Tamar. Palaces, churches and other grand projects were built, not only in Tbilisi but also throughout the Georgian lands. Tributes were paid by buffer states. It is no exaggeration to state that Georgia became one of the main states and empires of the Middle Eastern region. Marco Polo, who travelled through Georgia in the early thirteenth century on his way to China, called Tbilisi '*a handsome city, around which are settlements and many fortified posts*'.

Under Queen Tamar cultural and economic affairs flourished. A type of parliament came into existence. In Georgian this is called *darbazi*. Some Georgians claim this to be the first example in history of an attempt to circumvent the divine right of kings. There is some truth in the claim as the Georgian darbazi predates by some twenty-five years or so the Magna Carta that the barons and churchmen of England forced King John to sign in 1215. Such was the influence of the darbazi that it forced Tamar to divorce her first husband Giorgi Rusi (Prince Yuri), a Russian by birth. Later in 1189 the Queen married David Soslan an Ossetian prince who was raised at the Georgian court.

Tbilisi found itself as a significant centre for trade along the silk route. Spices, carpets, and all the exotica of the east were sold at the city's bazaars. The square to the south of the Metechi Bridge was one of the main trading posts. Nearby is the site of a Caravansarai (now the Tbilisi History Museum), where traders would rest along their routes. Tbilisi was now a multinational city and with traders passing through not only from the east and west but from the Dagestinian mountains in the north and from the Middle Eastern and Armenian lands to the south, one cannot help but imagine the haggling, noise, and air of wonder at the multitude of

*Queen Tamar,
contemporary icon painting*

languages being spoken as business was conducted. Georgian was the language of ecclesiastical life and the royal court but it is more than likely that Arabic and Persian were the main languages of trade.

Yet it was in the field of culture that we can still see glimpses of the Georgian golden age. King David moved the royal throne from the Narikala Fortress to the opposite bank of the Mtkvari River and under Queen Tamar an extensive palace was built on the site of what is now the ruins of Queen Darejan's Palace. The first construction of the Metechi Church was completed during Tamar's reign.

Writing, both ecclesiastical and secular developed. For Georgians their most celebrated writer to this day remains Shota Rustaveli who composed The Knight in the Panther Skin, an epic of courtly love and triumph against adversity. It was written as an ode to the great queen. Through the ages much has been written by Georgians and others on the beauty of the piece – a work that has stood the test of time and one that school children today still learn to recite. Artisan skills attained new heights. Throughout the country and capital, churches were adorned with frescoes – some exist to this day and there are many examples of book illumination in Tbilisi's Institute of Manuscripts. Additionally traditions of Georgia – metal chasing and gold decorative arts flourished. Beka Opizari was one of the more famous exponents of these arts.

THIRTEENTH TO THE NINETEENTH CENTURY

The Golden Age was cut abruptly short by a new danger from the East. Tamar's successor Giorgi Lasha, the Resplendent (1213-1222) was about to set forth upon a crusade and link with his Western European Christian allies. However a messenger from his own court returned from a sortie to announce to the king 'the arrival of a strange people, speaking an unknown tongue'. The Mongols had launched a campaign into the Caucasus and had already swept Armenia under their control. Giorgi Lasha gathered some ninety thousand horsemen against the new enemy, but was defeated. The Mongols pulverised all that stood before them and following their third attack sacked Tbilisi in 1236.

The Mongols exacted a heavy tribute from the Georgian kings. The economy began to decline and the glories of the past two hundred years became but memories as Tbilisi withered and declined under foreign rule. In the fifteenth century the Ottoman Turks moved into the Western Caucasus and by the end of that century Safavid Iran controlled the areas adjacent to the Caspian Sea. For local Georgian rulers the survival of any type of Georgian state and their own position involved seeking deals with their overlords and gaining small amounts of influence by playing off one against the other at moments of weakness. Events far removed from Tbilisi and the Caucasus also caused further deterioration. The Renaissance and the Age of Discovery in Western Europe opened up new sea based trade routes and left the old silk route to wither. Commercial decline affected local artisans and craftsmen. The combined factors of foreign dominion and a lack of trade reduced Tbilisi's importance and size. Georgians returned to the countryside that they had left some centuries before. By the end of the fifteenth century there were no more than ten thousand inhabitants resident in the capital.

Tbilisi emerged as a distinguished city once again only in the eighteenth century and mainly through the skills of two kings. Firstly there was Vakhtang VI (1703-1724). Vakhtang started his career as a regent before becoming king. He organised the systematic

King Luarsab, Queen Ketevan & King Demetre - fresco in Lower Bethlehem Church

collection of Georgian laws and introduced printing into the country. As a consequence not only the laws, but also Rustaveli's poem and the *Kartlis Tskovreba* (the chronicles of the history of Georgia) quickly became more accessible to a wider public.

It was not until the reign of Erekle II (1762-1798) that something of a Georgian state proper redeveloped. Writers on the history of the country have pointed out that Erekle's kingdom was a product of his own imagination and was a curious hybrid of tacking on pieces of land that he won over. Nevertheless, if initially he held his capital in Kakheti at Telavi, by 1762 he was able to reassert Tbilisi as the dominant city of a unified eastern Georgia.

Throughout the latter part of the eighteenth century, Georgian kings and noblemen increasingly looked north to Russia for protection against the encircling world of Islam that they saw around them. Erekle sought alliance with Catherine the Great of Russia but to little avail. Under the Treaty of Georgievsk signed in 1783, Russia promised to make Eastern Georgia a protectorate. Erekle's thinking was less a matter of wishing to be a part of Russia *per se* but more that the Christian north would offer more propitious opportunities for survival than either Iran or the Ottoman Turkey. However Catherine rescinded on the agreement and pulled out those Russian troops that were garrisoned in Erekle's kingdom following the out-break of the Russo-Turkish war of 1787.

Erekle was alone. In Iran a particularly cruel shah had ascended the throne, a certain Agha Shah Mohammed Khan. In 1795 he massed an army and invaded much of the Caucasus and sacked Tbilisi, burning it to the ground. As a consequence many of the architectural monuments of the city were destroyed. Some histori-ans argue that only the Narikala Fortress and the Anchiskhati Basilica survived the Persian onslaught. Despite the fact that Russia had seemingly abandoned Erekle at his hour of need, his successors still sought alliance with the northern neighbour. The last king of Eastern Georgia, Giorgi XII wrote to General Lazarev, commander of the Russian forces: 'Our blood belongs to his Imperial Majesty, and we have sworn this with our last drop of blood'.

RUSSIAN CONQUEST AND SOVIET CONTROL

In 1801, Tsar Alexander I unilaterally decided that Russia's interests were best served by incorporating the Caucasus into the Russian Empire. Tbilisi and its hinterland of Eastern Georgia was the first area to fall under Russian rule. Under the Treaties of Gulistan of 1812 and Turkmenchai in 1828 the whole southern Caucasus region became fully part of Russia. The Georgian royal family was abol-ished. If Georgia had hoped that Russia would bring protection from their Muslim neighbours they could not have conceived that this would mean complete control. As Prince Garsevan Chavchavadze wrote at the time: 'They have abolished our king-dom...No country has been so humiliated as Georgia'.

Thus it was that a two hundred year association with Russia began. Controversy still remains concerning whether Russian influ-ence was beneficial or otherwise. On a human level, relations between Russians and Georgians have always been and no doubt will continue to be good. However on a state level there have always been difficulties. This tension was benign for long periods but at specific instances led to outright revolt and conflict.

Russia's arrival in the capital signalled considerable change not only to the landscape of the city but also to its organisation. While Georgia the country was officially abolished, along with the monar-chy and the church, Tbilisi or Tiflis as the Russians termed it, became the centre for the whole Caucasus region. Within the city in the early nineteenth century the old town was rebuilt. Under the direction of Mikhail Semenovich Vorontsov (Viceroy from 1845-1854), the Georgian noblemen and Armenian merchants developed plans and brought to fruition a major expansion of the city.

In 1848, most of the old walls of the city were removed and the city began to expand northwards and westwards. An area called Garetubani that is now Rustaveli Avenue and Freedom Square was

*Artists view of Tbilisi in the
nineteenth century*

designated as the centre of the city. Elegant three storey mansions
were built along the avenue as well as palaces and churches. A theatre and an opera house were erected. What has become the main
thoroughfare of the city Rustaveli Avenue was named Golovinsky
Avenue initially and the city's central square now Freedom Square
was first named Paskevich-Erevansky Square in honour of Graf
Paskevich Erevansky who was commander in chief of the Russian
forces during the Russian-Turkish war and conquered Erevan Castle
in 1829. Later the square's name was shortened to Erevan Square.

As the century progressed so the numbers of people migrating
to the city increased. Archival figures inform that in 1811 the population of the city was a mere 8,500. By 1825 the population had
more than doubled to 20,000 and as the century drew to a close in
1897 the city could boast some 169,000 inhabitants.

Russian rule exposed the townsfolk of Tbilisi to not only Russian
culture and ideas but also those of France, Germany, Italy and
Britain. A new generation of writers and thinkers emerged under
colonial rule. Akaki Tsereteli and Ilia Chavchavadze are but two and
perhaps the most famous associated with the developing nineteenth century national movement.

The arts advanced particularly in the latter part of the nineteenth century. Great Russian and Western European writers,
Dumas, Pushkin, Tolstoy, Lermontov and others journeyed to Tbilisi
and drew inspiration from the Caucasus mountains and the charm

21

of the capital. To many a writer and artist Tbilisi became the Paris of the east.

As the twentieth century dawned so also increasingly did the notion that Georgians should take more control over their lives. Following the First World War, Georgia was able to declare itself an independent country (1918-1921). Unfortunately it was short-lived. Events external to the country, the lack of assistance from countries such as Britain and Germany left the country to be invaded or 'incorporated' into what became the Soviet Union. For the last time in its history Tbilisi was ruled and controlled from afar. Any consideration of the Soviet period is going to be controversial, particularly as most of the residents of the city today lived for a part of if not most of their lives under that system. Nevertheless the city changed considerably through the twentieth century. Distinguishing between what was Soviet intent and the perhaps natural development of a large city is almost impossible.

Nevertheless there are a few features that can be picked out. In both population size and territorial extent Tbilisi increased enormously. In 1920 the land area of the city was some fifty three square kilometres. By the nineteen eighties the city had increased some ten times in size to three hundred and sixty five square kilometres. In 1920 the population of Tbilisi was 11 percent of the whole country. In 1989 this figure had increased to nearly 25 percent, making the capital a more dominant component in the life of the country than London to Britain or Paris to France. The march towards rapid industrialisation in the nineteen thirties followed later by demands brought upon by the Second World War brought the location of heavy industry to the capital and with it large scale movements of people from rural areas. Specific features of the Soviet system such as the command economy and centralised planning exacerbated the growth. Thus villages such as Gldani, Mukhiani and Orkhevi were progressively incorporated into the city – their feature today being large-scale apartment blocks traditional of Soviet cities.

In the old town and centre the effect of Soviet rule was mixed. The demands of socialist planning and ideology meant that some churches were pulled down and replaced by monoliths to Soviet architecture. The site of the Parliament of the country is but one example. Additionally charming old quarters were demolished. Republican Square with its military style parade ground is a case in point. At the same time parts of the old town were lovingly restored to their former glory. The balconied houses on Baratashvili Street and the Sulphur Bath complex are two such sites.

TBILISI TODAY

In 1991 Tbilisi found itself at the head of an independent state that could look forward to ruling itself in the modern age that we now live in. The past ten years or so have not been easy on the city.

A view towards the Old Town

There has been a period of civil strife that damaged part of the centre. Conflicts that plagued the country in the early years of the nineteen nineties forced large numbers of people to seek sanctuary in the capital. Still many of the major Soviet built hotels are home to refugees from those bloody and unfortunate wars. Additionally the transition to a market economy has left parts of the city looking a little unkempt. However at the same time organisations have grown to protect and develop the city's character and infrastructure.

Above all perhaps Tbilisi and all those that live in the city share an indomitable spirit. This spirit that has withstood some twenty nine invasions down the centuries has kept Tbilisi alive. As stability returns to the country at large and with the shoots of economic recovery increasingly evident, so the city is starting to prosper once more. Yet today Tbilisi is able to develop and grow on its own terms. It retains its highly cosmopolitan nature but is the essential heart of Georgia. Tbilisians as the city folk term themselves celebrate their city in song and through festivals. In autumn each year a weekend is devoted to the celebration of the city through the festival of *Tbilisoba*.

Arguments continue as to whether Tbilisi is a Middle Eastern or European city. It is both and neither. For Tbilisi is the beating heart of Georgia and the wider Caucasus, with its own particular rhythm and soul. By exploring the sites of the capital, wandering through the maze of streets of the old town, dining out on traditional cuisine and most of all mixing with the city folk one will soon discover the true essence of Tbilisi. For it is as its name implies the place of warmth.

Panorama of the City

THE OLD TOWN

METECHI CHURCH, SACHINO PALACE, SULPHUR BATHS, BOTANICAL
GARDENS, NARIKALA FORTRESS

A suitable starting point to begin to discover Tbilisi is perhaps
with one of the major landmarks, the **Metechi Church** that rests
upon the top of the cliff over looking the Mtkvari River. The statue
adjacent to the church is of the city's founder king Vakhtang
Gorgasali. It was designed by Elguja Amashukeli in 1958 to mark
the 1,500 anniversary of the capital. King Vakhtang Gorgasali commissioned one of the very first Christian churches in Tbilisi to be
built here. The Metechi Church of today was built in 1289 under
the orders of Demetre II (the Devoted). King Demetre ruled Eastern
Georgia at the time when the Mongols controlled the country. By
careful alliance with the Mongol il-Khan overlords, he was able to
restore some of the privileges that the Georgian Church had lost
when the Mongols first invaded. However in the internecine strug-
gles between the Mongols, Demetre backed the wrong side, but to
protect his capital from invasion and destruction he agreed to sur-
render and be executed.

Before Demetre ordered the church to be built, this site was
both religious and royal. David the Builder had his royal palace here
and this is also where Queen Tamar married her second husband
David Soslan. Both the palace and original church were destroyed
during the Mongol's invasion in 1235. The palace was rebuilt some
years after the church, the latter being for a long period the royal
chapel. It is believed that some of the stones used to build the thirteenth century church were those of the earlier church dating from
the fifth century. In the seventeenth century the church was again
partially destroyed by the Turks. During Erekle II's reign in 1748 the
church was repaired to its former glory, only to be destroyed once
again along with the palace during Shah Agha Mohammed Khan's
destruction of Tbilisi in 1795. Under Russian rule the site was the
home of the infamous Metechi Jail. This was removed in 1937. In
the latter part of the Soviet period the church lost its religious purpose and was used as a theatre. However with independence for
the country as a whole, the Metechi church has rightly regained its
religious nature.

The Metechi is a cross in square church made of both brick and
dressed stone. The eastern part of the church has three projecting
apses, a feature somewhat uncommon for its period. The brick
dome was built in 1748 under the guidance of Erekle II. The façade
is generally smooth. The most decorative part is in the eastern
apses around the windows. Unfortunately the period of Russification
in the nineteenth century has left the walls white-washed. It is
believed there are some interesting frescoes beneath. The icons that

Metechi Church

are dotted throughout the church are all Georgian orthodox. On the far wall from the entrance is an imposing copy of a fresco of Queen Tamar.

In a small side chapel to the right of the altar is the tomb of Saint Shushanik. *The Martyrdom of Saint Shushanik* remains the oldest surviving work of Georgian literature. The narrative was com-

posed between the years 476 and 483 by Jacob of Tsurtaveli and is remarkable for its directness of language. It recounts the story of Shushanik who refused to submit to her husband's order to convert to Zoroastrianism. He beat her and locked her in a cell on this site but she never lost her Christian faith. It could be argued and has been that Saint Shushanik was an early example of feminism in

Left - Echmiadzin Church
Top - Baptism in the Metechi Church
Above - Tomb of Saint Shushanik in the Metechi Church

27

Church of the Transfiguration

Georgia. Still today many Armenian girls – for Shushanik was an ethnic Armenian – are named after this saint beloved of both the Georgians and Armenians.

Leaving the Metechi Church complex, the road leading up the hill to the right of the souvenir shop is called Metechi Rise. The houses on your right date from the nineteenth century, one being now a diplomatic residence. At the foot of the rise is one of Tbilisi's many theatres the Old House Theatre. Metechi Rise winds through to Metechi Street that meets Ketevan the Martyr Avenue (*Ketevan Tsamebulis Gamziri*). An underpass close by allows one to visit the Armenian **Echmiadzin Church**. This church was built in 1804 by refugees from Echmiadzin in Armenia. The brown obelisk style monument in front of the church is dedicated from the Armenian nation to those Georgians who perished at the hands of Soviet troops on April 9th 1989. The interior of the church is less than spectacular, partly because significant damage was caused by flooding from the underground water table, during excavation work for the nearby metro station in the latter part of the Soviet period. The central dome has frescoes dating from the nineteenth century of Matthew, Mark, Luke and John. Many of the icons are not Armenian but rather eastern orthodox and catholic. The local priest explains their presence as an indication of the ecumenical and democratic nature of the Armenian Church.

To the right of the entrance door in the corner is an Armenian icon of Saint Vardan. Vardan lived in the fifth century and was the father of the beloved martyr Shushanik. In 451 the Persians waged war against Armenian princes after a series of attempts to force the Armenians to follow Zoroastrianism. Under the leadership of Vardan Mamikonian, these princes fought against the might of the Persian Empire. This battle, known as the Battle of Avarayr is the first recorded battle in defence of Christianity. The battle became a spiritual victory for the Armenians, even though they actually lost, because the Persian kings recognised their claims for freedom of worship. Armenians hold Saint Vardan in great respect. Even today Armenian children will recite the phrase "*I am Armenian; I am the grandchild of Brave Vardan.*"

Crossing the main road or using the underpass, there are two routes back to the old town proper. The steep cobbled alley is called Wine Rise (*Ghvinis Aghmarti*). Many streets in this part of the town retain their old names reflecting the market trading nature of the city. Wine Rise is where one could in previous centuries always find the main wine producers from mainly the Kakhetian region in the east of the country selling their produce in the capital. Today there are still one or two wine cellars (*dukani*) on the street as well as murals showing a Georgian man with his drinking horn (*khantsi*), a collection of minstrels and a reproduction of a painting by one of Tbilisi's most celebrated artists Pirosmani. (See the museums section for details about him.) For those who do not wish to descend only to walk up again, take Metechi Street the first road on the right from leaving the underpass. Peristzvaleba Street the second on the right leads to the **Sachino Palace**. Just before turning right you can see the ruins of a nineteenth century Armenian Church called Shamkhorets.

Above - Frescoes in the Church of the Transfiguration

The remains of the palace one sees today are some two hundred years old. Erekle II, the last but one king of Georgia, had the palace built as a summer residence for his Queen in 1776. The palace was built within the walls of the Avlabari Fortress that was built at an earlier period. There are two names for this royal complex. Sachino means eminent. This is a reference not only to the royal family but also the site's location. The other appellation is Queen Darejan's Palace. One can imagine the Queen looking out over the city during the summer months from the wooden balcony that remains to this day. Darejan's palace was rather modest. Indeed this appears to be a feature in Georgia of the royal family. If in many cultures rulers would have constructed imposing palaces and edifices, in Georgia this is singularly absent. Part of the reason for this may be the fact that for long periods local rulers, in trying to fend off invasion, were on the move and at least not based in the capital. Another explanation may lie in the numerous churches that exist not only in Tbilisi but also throughout the country. The kings and queens of Georgia decided that honouring God was preferable to surrounding themselves in majesty.

Today Sachino is notable for what one can see from it. The views of the old city are simply stunning. There is perhaps no better vantage point than to sit on the balcony and survey the city. In the spring and early summer all the greens imaginable are represented with the trees dotted through the tiny squares of the old town directly in front. To the left stands the Narikala Fortress while to the right is the centre of Tbilisi with the backdrop of Mtatsminda Mountain. In the autumn months the colours change to auburn and brown while in winter it appears as though the city is almost colourless.

The church on this site is called the **Church of the Transfiguration**. It was originally built in 1776 and named after King Erekle and Queen Darejan and used as their royal chapel. In the nineteenth century it was substantially redesigned. Today it functions as a church in its own right, and indeed the whole complex is considered a holy place. The interior of the church has frescoes that date from the early twentieth century.

Moving back down the slope, the Metechi Bridge leads into the Kala district. The original bridge (the first such in Tbilisi) had two watchtowers at either end. In 1870 it was replaced by a metal bridge the first of its type in Tbilisi and designed by the British engineer Ordysh. During the Soviet period it was replaced by the current span. During mediaeval times this provided the main route into Tbilisi, as the city walls extended down from the Narikala to the river. Still on the northern bank of the river the open space to the right is called Riqe. Today it is used as a parade ground and is where the annual city fair Tbilisoba is concentrated. The small huts house restaurants reflecting the regional cuisine of the country. In the nineteenth century Riqe was particularly prone to flooding. In 1893 and 1896 the area was plunged completely under water and many buildings were destroyed, although it was in the nineteen sixties that the district took upon the character that one can see today.

The square immediately in front on the other side of the river is called Gorgasali Square. Previously it was called Maidan Square and Castle Square. During the seventeenth and eighteenth centuries the main market of the city was located here called Sheytan (Devil's) Bazaar. As such it was one of the main trading sites along the Silk Route. On the right hand side was a sixteenth century mosque

Sachino Palace

pulled down by the Soviets in the nineteen forties. Indeed much of the square was considerably redesigned during the Soviet period. Previously the square was closed off.

Above the square is **Saint Gevork** (Saint George) – now an Armenian Cathedral, most of which dates from 1251. However Georgian sources and chronicles call the church Tsikhis Didi Eklesia literally meaning the Fortress's Large Church predating its Armenian

31

Balconied houses above the Mtkvari River

appellation. In early mediaeval times there was a castle here built and controlled by the Persians. After the Persians were banished from the city in 1748, the church that stands today was transferred to the Armenian Church in 1780. Sayat Nova, a famous eighteenth century ashug, a type of minstrel poet, is buried in the courtyard of the cathedral. There is a monument to him to the right of the main door of the church. The interior of Saint Gevork has a few frescoes and was considerably renovated some twenty years ago.

Turning right outside St. Gevork, Samghebro Street with some noticeable balconied houses descends to Bath (*Abano*) Street, home as the name suggests of Tbilisi's famous **Sulphur Baths**. The brick domes on the left of the street host the main baths of the city. The baths are fed by natural hydrogen sulphide water from underground springs and have a curative effect. While this is the principal area of springs in the city, it is not exclusively so. In some of the suburbs residential homes are linked to the capital's underground mineral water riches.

The oldest baths are the Erekle Baths, the first baths on the left. Historians attest that the original baths probably date from the Arab period (seventh-eighth century). During the Golden Age there were some sixty eight baths altogether, but by the seventeenth century, following successive invasion and destruction the figure reduced to

Saint Gevork Armenian Cathedral

just six. The impressive Islamic looking building at the far end of the street is called the Orbeliani Bathhouse named after the Orbeliani family. The mosaic style façade is the last surviving example of Islamic influence upon the city. The building dates from the late seventeenth century but was significantly restored during both the nineteenth and twentieth centuries. The Orbeliani bath is communal and so if one wants to test out the recuperating powers of the

Above Right - Bath Street
Above - Orbeliani Baths Detail
Below - Minaret of the Mosque

waters, and to relax in privacy the Erekle baths are a better bet. By doing so you will be in good company. For almost all travellers to Tbilisi whether famous or not have undergone this unforgettable experience. The plaque to the left of the Orbeliani Bathhouse reveals the thoughts of Alexander Pushkin, *'I have never in my life come across anything better than the baths in Tiflis'.* An interesting feature, if you are lucky enough to choose the correct one, is a statue of Pushkin in one of the compartments of the Erekle Baths.

If you decide upon a bath it is advisable to set aside around three hours – and take a swimming costume with you. Make sure as well after your bath that you request a cup of tea. As Peter the Great of Russia mentioned *'Sell your white stockings if you have to but have tea after your bath'.*

Having taken in the sulphur baths return down the street, and take the next alley left at the corner where there is a shop selling carpets. The narrow cobbled street is called Botanical Street and leads to both the Botanical Gardens and Narikala Fortress. Some fifty metres up the street is the only Mosque in Tbilisi. It dates from the nineteenth century and mainly serves the local Azeri community who live in the neighbouring streets. A distinctive feature of the old town is how closely together the different communities live. There may have been trouble between the differing nationalities of the Caucasus since the fall of communism but this has not had any impact upon the old town.

At the top of Botanical Street are the gates of the **Botanical Gardens**. The Gardens opened to the public in 1845, having previously been the preserve of the Georgian royal family in the seven-

The Sulphur Baths

teenth and early eighteenth centuries. Unfortunately the gardens suffered in the early days of independence but are now better protected. There is nevertheless something of a shortage of money for maintenance and development, although it is hoped that it may soon regain its former glories. In its heyday, the Botanical Gardens boasted some 5,000 different species of plants drawn not only from the Caucasus but also from other parts of the world. The area covered is some 128 hectares and situated as it is on the Sololaki Range it is possible to leave Tbilisi completely. Indeed it just possible to continue walking over the hills to the Krtsanisi region where the President of Georgia now has his official residence.

From a number of key look out points, the Botanical Gardens offer stunning views over the rest of the city. There are two exit points to the gardens. The best way is through the main gates where you entered. The other way out is through a tunnel that is normally without light and a little dank. Upon leaving the gardens return down Botanical Street until you see a set of steps on the left. These lead to the **Narikala Fortress**. Alternatively one can return back down towards river level and from the back of Saint Gevork

Botanical Street

Cathedral at its left side from the river, take Salmi Street up to the main gate of the fortress. The road is fairly steep but also affords good views of the city below.

Standing imposingly over the old town, on the top of Sololaki Hill, the Narikala Fortress (also known as Shuris Tsikhe – the Rival

Botanical Gardens

Fortress) dates from the fourth century. It was probably first erected by the Persians but has been added to and modified by most rulers down the centuries. Vakhtang Gorgasali when converting the nation's capital from Mtskheta to Tbilisi built upon the original Persian design. This process continued in the reign of his son and heir Dachi. Much of what we see today dates from when the Arabs controlled Tbilisi. Both the upper and lower parts of the fortress date from the eighth century. With its unique strategic advantage both local rulers and foreign invaders looked to make Narikala their headquarters. At the western extent of the complex, the Shakhtakhti Tower dates from between the seventh and ninth centuries. It was built as an observatory. The Arab built a palace within

Top - Bells of Saint Nicholas Church

Above - Narikala Fortress Detail

Right - Saint Nicholas Church

the walls of Narikala and this was situated adjacent to the Shakhtakhti Tower.

King David the Builder moved the city's royal palace to the opposite bank of the river in the Avlabari region in the twelfth century. Nevertheless he recognised the significance of Narikala and added additional fortifications. Successive invaders, Mongols, Persians and Turks added and modified to the original structure. The tower at the furthest southwest extent is called the Istanbul tower. It was built in the sixteenth century during what is termed the *Osmanloba* (1723-1735), a brief yet terrible period, when the Ottomans held control of the capital and used the tower as a prison.

Narikala Fortress

The ruins we see today are the result not of invasion. Rather, in 1827 the whole fortress exploded when gunpowder stored by the Russian military was set alight by a bolt of lightening. As a consequence it is difficult to grasp today the full extent of the complex. Yet from the ramparts there are extraordinary views of the city.

Archaeological research in 1967 revealed that there was a twelfth century church inside the Narikala complex. In 1982 repair works started on the fortress and as Georgia became independent once again, the Patriarch of Georgia Ilia II, with the blessing of the government commissioned the rebuilding of **Saint Nicholas Church**. The church was finished in 1996 and was designed in keeping with the fortress surrounding it. Parts of the walls are made

Narikala Fortress from the Botanical Gardens

up from the stonework of the original church. The interior is completely decorated with frescoes, depicting both biblical scenes and from the history of Georgia.

THE HEART OF KALA

ANCHISKHATI, SIONI, CARAVANSARAI, JVARISMAMA, NORASHEN, UPPER & LOWER BETHLEHEM, MOGHNIN, SURP NISHAN

Baratashvili Street provides the starting point to explore the heart of the old town. Here there are numerous examples of Tbilisi's famous balconies. Both the balconied houses and the city walls are renovations carried out during the nineteen seventies and eighties. Before the bridge crosses the river on the right hand side is the start of Shavteli Street with a monument of an old man based upon *The Janitor* by Pirosmani. The other sculpture is called Berikaoba and was designed in 1981 by Avtandil Monselidze. The idea of the sculpture is to represent merrymakers dancing in a carnival procession. At number thirteen Shavteli Street is Rezo Gabriadze's famous Marionette Theatre. A few steps along Shavteli Street lies Tbilisi's oldest church called **Anchiskhati**. The church dates from the sixth century and is a typical representation of the period. Vakhtang Gorgasali's son Dachi Udjarmeli commissioned the building, when the plans for constructing the new capital were in full operation. Originally the church was dedicated to the Virgin Mary but in the seventeenth century took on the additional appellation of Anchiskhati following the movement of the Anchiskhati icon from the Monastery of Anchi in the southwest of the country. The icon itself dates from the twelfth century and is the work of a famous goldsmith of the period Beka Opizari. It is currently kept in the Museum of Georgian Art.

Anchiskhati is a basilica type church. The main middle nave leads to a horseshoe shaped altar apse. The accompanying side naves end in right angles. As with many of Tbilisi's churches Anchiskhati has undergone several changes most notably in the seventeenth century when the upper part of the church and several internal columns were refashioned in brick. The oldest parts of the church are the walls in stone, window frames on the eastern façade and the window above the altar. In 1958 considerable restoration work was enacted to return the church to how it must have looked in the sixth century. The floor was dropped to its original level. A

Above - The City Janitor on Shavteli Street based upon a Pirosmani painting

Below and Left - City walls and Balconies on Baratashvili Street

nineteenth century bell tower and a false dome on top of the basilica were removed. By removing the bell tower an interesting carved relief, in the shape of a symmetrical cross was revealed. Also, frescoes dating from the seventeenth century were uncovered.

Anchiskhati remains a hugely significant church for the Georgian Church. It is believed that at the time of Christ the king of Georgia of that period was ill. As a last resort two members of his household travelled to Jerusalem because they had heard of a man who could heal the sick. They returned from the Holy Land with the imprint of Jesus Christ on a towel. Once the king was shown the face of Christ he was healed. The shroud it is believed was kept at the spot where Anchiskhati now stands. The historical basis for this story is at best dubious, although the *Georgian Chronicles* mention that two Jews from Mtskheta performed this operation and that the shroud was brought back to the then capital of Georgia.

In front of the church is a double storey bell tower built in 1675, under the order of Catholicos Domenti of Georgia. The brickwork is Islamic in tone a reflection perhaps of the influence of the religion over the city during that period. The greyish blue stone of

Top - Doorway of Anchiskhati
Above - Gates of Anchiskhati
Right - Bell Tower of Anchiskhati
Opposite - Anchiskhati

the belfry on top suggests the work of a different architect from the structure below. The ground floor used to be a living quarter, the interior of which is decorated with arches and niches. The inscription above the gates states "*We, blessed by Christ the Prince, Catholicos Domenti built the present bell tower and restarted the present church in the memory of my soul when reigning over the Kartalania of Shahnavaz in 363*".

At the side of the church there is a small cloister where there are some good examples of Tbilisi's wooden balconies. Now used predominantly as offices including that of Caucasus Travel, they were in Domenti's time his living quarters as well as for his administration and retinue. Back on Shavteli Street the left hand building, following a number of small dwelling places is the **Patriarchy**. The front of the Patriarch of Georgia's official residence can be viewed by descending down Shavteli Descent towards the river. The building itself lies on the foundations of a seventeenth century royal palace built during the reign of King Rostom (1632-1658) the only remains of which are a brick bathhouse. The palace was destroyed during Agha Shah Mohammed Khan's sacking of Tbilisi in 1795.

The Patriarch is the spiritual and temporal head of the Georgian Orthodox Church. When Georgia adopted Christianity in the fourth century the Church of Kartli was under the jurisdiction of the Apostolic See of Antioch. During the reign of King Vakhtang Gorgasali, through the intercession of the Byzantine Emperor and the Patriarch of Constantinople, the Patriarchy of Antioch granted self-governance (autocephaly) to the Church of Kartli and elevated the Bishop of Mtskheta to the rank of Catholicos. In Western Georgia the Church of Abkhazeti was under the rule of the Patriarch of Constantinople but there too autocephaly was introduced. When the country united in the eleventh century the Catholicos of Mtskheta (Kartli) was elevated to the position of Patriarch and from that time forth the head of the Georgian Church has carried the title of Catholicos-Patriarch of All Georgia. In 1811 Russia abolished the autocephaly of the church and the Georgian Church became subject to the rule of the Russian Church. In 1917 as Georgia moved towards independence the autocephaly of the Church and the patriarchate was briefly re-established. In 1943 to help ensure that Georgians would participate in the war effort, Stalin ordered the church's autocephaly to be restored. Since 1977 the Catholicos-Patriarch and Archbishop of Mtskheta - Tbilisi has been Ilia II.

On the right hand side of Shavteli Street is a small rose garden and the **Church of Saint George**. This was the site of one of Tbilisi's largest churches during the early mediaeval period. It was however destroyed in the fourteenth century Mongol invasion of Georgia. In 1645 King Rostom of Eastern Georgia ordered the building of three churches from the remains of the original. Only the Church of Saint George still exists. Building was completed under the direction of Prince Svimon in 1710. The façades that are visible today date from the nineteenth century, while the bell tower is late twentieth century.

Shavteli Street leads to Erekle II Square. This square that used to be called Royal Square and was formerly much larger is a perfect spot for quiet contemplation. With further examples of balconies and residential quarters, this provides a suitable point to mention something of the style of housing in the Old Town. Much of the layout of the Old Town preserves its mediaeval shape, although the buildings themselves date predominantly from the nineteenth century. Following the destruction of much of the city in 1795 new residential quarters were built upon existing foundations or upon the ruins of remaining structures. This is in marked contrast to the city centre and other districts where nineteenth century construction followed distinct new plans. Before Shah Agha Mohammed Khan's destruction of Tbilisi in 1795 there were two types of housing called *baniani sakhli* and *darbazi*. Characteristic of the *darbazi* was the placement of a hearth in the middle of a hall-type dwelling, with holes for light to come in and smoke to escape at the top of the

Shavteli Street

45

Top - Bell Tower, Church of Saint George

Right - Saint George Church and Rose Garden

Page 44, Top - The Patriarchy

Bottom Left - Wrought Iron Staircase

Bottom Right - Balcony on Shavteli Street

roof. In the *baniani sakhli* the hearth was replaced by a fireplace with a full smokestack and windows to let in the light. Examples of these types of houses can be seen in the Ethnographic Museum.

By the nineteenth century the style of housing changed. Two storey and occasionally three storey houses were erected with suites of rooms opening onto a common open balcony. In many cases the size of the balcony was the same as the floor area of the rooms. Balconies became the principle decorative feature of the house and were often reached by an outside, often wrought iron spiralled staircase. The balconies suggest a passing nod to Persian and Ottoman styles but are intrinsically Georgian. In many quarters the dwelling houses centre upon a small courtyard.

In the south east of the square is Erekle II Street that leads to Sioni Street and the spiritual home for Tbilisians, **Sioni Cathedral**. The original church was started in 500 during the reign of King Guaram of Iberia. It was finished in 620 when King Adarnese I ruled. The cathedral has been ransacked, and damaged many times through its history. The original dome of the cathedral was destroyed following the invasion of the city by Jalal al-Din in 1226. Successive invaders, Tamarlaine in the fourteenth century and the Persians under Shah Ismail in 1522 and Shah Abbas in the seventeenth century again caused damage. In the eighteenth century the conquering Turks even attempted to turn the cathedral into a mosque. Despite all the havoc and destruction Sioni has survived and in such terms may be judged as a symbol for the city as a whole. The general structure dates from Georgia's Golden Age in the thirteenth century. Each time the building has been damaged,

renovation work has brought it back to its previous state or added to it. Under the direction of archbishop Elisei Saghinashvili in 1657 a southern chapel was added as well as extensive renovation of the cupola. The inscription at the southern door testifies to Saghinashvili's work. It reads "*By the will of God and with the help of the Sioni Blessed Virgin Mary, I the metropolate Elisei Saghinashvili of Tbilisi, built Sioni's dome, the side walls and the door, painted and decorated with all possible adornments. Forgive Me. Amen. Chronicon 345, (1657)*".

Some sixty years later in 1710 during the reign of Vakhtang VI, many of the exterior walls were restored and the dome rebuilt. In the early nineteenth century further renovation was conducted as a result of which the western façade was coated and in 1826 damaged frescoes were restored. In 1860 extensive interior work was carried out. Using the designs of Grigory Gagarin the whole church was repainted. Gagarin was a notable Russian painter, architect and diplomat who not only displayed his talents in Sioni but also composed a number of landscapes of Tbilisi. His works adorn a number of editions of Alexandre Dumas' celebrated account of his adventures in the Caucasus, *Impressions de Voyage au Caucase*. Today Gagarin's frescoes are visible in the upper parts of the cathedral. The frescoes decorating the lower walls are very modern. These were completed in 1989 and are the work of Levan Tsutskiridze. All the icons in the cathedral are Georgian. The most recent is of Ilia Chavchavadze a celebrated writer of the nineteenth century who was canonised in the late nineteen eighties.

Top - Tbilisi Seminary
Right - Bell Tower,
Sioni Cathedral

Page 45, Top - Balcony near
the Mtkvari River
Bottom Left - Nikoloz
Baratashvili Museum
Bottom Right - Fountain
Erekle II Square

Sioni Cathedral

Sioni is representative of a typical cross in square construction with a developed eastern part with prominent granite apses. The dome is situated on vaults abutting from the altar walls and two further columns that allude to the shape of an arrow. This particular design is probably the result of the renovation work in the seventeenth century. The exterior walls have limited or restricted ornamentation apart from the dome itself that is more elaborate. In 1978 the Patriarch of Georgia approved limited excavation works. This uncovered hidden layers and some of the original stonework.

*Sioni Cathedral from
the Mtkvari River*

One of the most venerated objects of the Georgian Church is held in Sioni. This is the Cross of Saint Nino. Saint Nino is credited with bringing Christianity to Georgia in the fourth century. She hailed from Cappadocia and left Jerusalem to seek out Christ's crucifixion coat. Under the guidance of a vision from the Virgin Mary she believed the cloak to be held in Mtskheta. According to the Georgian Chroniclers she arrived in Georgia with only a cross made of the sinuous branches of the vine bound by her own hair. After performing a number of miracles including saving the life of King

Russian Bell Tower

Mirian of Iberia, the country converted to Christianity. The cross that you can see is a replica of the original also kept in the church behind the iconostasis.

The bell tower to the left of the entrance to Sioni is late medi-aeval. It is difficult to ascribe a precise date. Some authors suggest 1425 but this is now considered erroneous. There are three storeys but all but the base floor were destroyed during Shah Agha Mohammed Khan's destruction of the city in 1795. It was restored in 1939. The bell is still struck to call believers to prayer. If you visit when the bell chimes it cannot fail to leave an indelible impression.

The Synagogue interior

Over the road the white bell tower dates from the early nineteenth century and is the oldest example of Russian classicism in the city. Today the bottom part of the tower serves as a theological bookshop. Next door to the bell tower is The Tbilisi Theological Seminary converted from an old caravansarai.

Continuing down the street on the right is a shop selling souvenirs of the Georgian Orthodox Church. Next door and down a steep flight of steps is one of Tbilisi's famous bakeries called *Tone*. Here you can see bread being baked in the traditional manner as well as sample khachapuri. Immediately opposite is Tbilisi's

Jvarismama Church

Caravansarai. Today it houses the Tbilisi Historical Museum (details of which you can find in the museum section of this guide). The building is essentially a nineteenth century reconstruction of the seventeenth century original. The river side façade dates from 1820 while that of the street side is some one hundred years later. The roofing of what would have been the courtyard is a result of work in the nineteen eighties. The interior is a traditional design for a caravansarai. The three balconied floors would have been divided into rooms for dining, entertaining and sleeping, while what is now

Norashen

the basement would have been the area for resting horses and camels.

A small wander along Sioni Street takes you up to the cobbled Leselidze Street. This is the main street of the old city connecting, the Metechi Bridge to Freedom Square. As you ascend from Sioni Cathedral on the opposite side of the street is the **Iulo Synagogue** built in 1910. Georgian Jewish relations go back over two thousand five hundred years and have always been positive. There is no evidence of anti-semitism in Georgia. It is believed for example a

Right - Mother Georgia

Below - Saint George's Church on the Rock Detail

Far Right - Saint George's Church on the Rock

Far Right Bottom - Saint George's Church on the Rock Detail

Jewish man brought the cloak of Jesus from Palestine to Bethlehem in the first century AD. Jews in Georgia are divided between what are called Georgian Jews who have been in the country since time immemorial and speak Georgian and Jews who came to Georgia in the nineteenth and twentieth century from other parts of Eastern Europe and who tend to speak Russian. The synagogue itself has two floors. For most of the Soviet period the lower floor was closed. The upper part was sealed off but remained open for worship for those in the know. To protect themselves from the authorities the Torah was bound inside copies of Marx and Lenin should there ever be a raid! Since the nineteen seventies many of Tbilisi's Jewish community emigrated to Israel. However the synagogue remains the centre of the community and the shops around you will see contain kosher products.

Along Leselidze Street to the left there are two churches. The smaller church is Georgian and is called **Jvarismama** or Father of the Cross. The original here was started in the fifth century and was added to in the eleventh and mainly in the sixteenth centuries. Both the Mongols in the thirteenth century and later the Persians in

1795 destroyed Jvarismama. The building of today has some features from the sixteenth century as well as from extensive work conducted in 1825. The name of the church derives from the fact that its main function was to serve monks returning from Jerusalem. In Jerusalem there is a Georgian monastery called Saint Cross that takes its name from Jvarismama. The frescoes in the dome above the altar date from the sixteenth century. There are plans afoot to add more frescoes and to extend the church. For part of its history Jvarismama was a Greek Orthodox Church serving the small Greek population of Tbilisi. The icons are contemporary and depict Saint Nicholas, The Virgin Mary, Jesus Christ and Saint Nino. The façades of the church are partially decorated with brick crosses.

Next door is the Armenian church called Norashen. The name means new building. It was built on the site of an earlier church. The current building dates from 1793. **Norashen** contains the best examples of Armenian frescoes in Tbilisi but unfortunately is normally closed. Today it is used as a library store. The frescoes date from the founding of the church and were painted by a celebrated Armenian artist, Ovt Natanian. A feature of particular interest is the

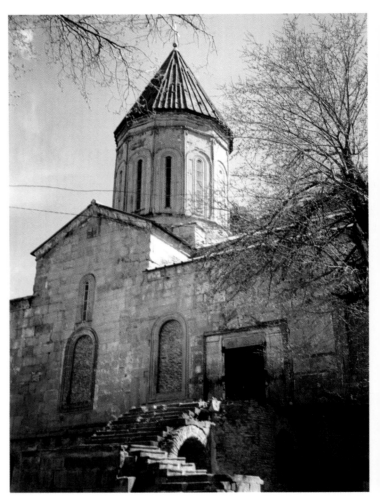

Top - Fresco, Lower Bethlehem Church

Right - Upper Bethlehem Church

Far Right - Lower Bethlehem Church

Far Right Bottom - Steps near the Lower Bethlehem Church

red colour called *vortan karmir* meaning the red worm. This comes from a special worm from the Ararat Valley in Armenia. It is also supposed to be the true colour used on the Armenian national flag.

Jerusalem Street at the side of Jvarismama leads towards Jerusalem Square and Bread Square (*puris moedani*). At this junction take the street called Askana. This is a small winding alley with a rather tumble down nature. However as one walks up through this area one can appreciate well the compactness of the old town. Noticeable as well are the balconies and tiny wrought iron staircases

that perch out precariously from various yards linking one house to another. A set of narrow steps leads up to Gomi Street. Turn left here and soon you should see a set of steps on the right. This is the only route to **Kldis Eklesia** or Saint George's Church on the Rock. The church is a basilica type and dates from the sixteenth century.

Retrace your steps back along Gomi Street. The remains of the **Ateshka Zoroastrian Temple** are on the left hand side of the street (a brick structure) opposite from a house with a large balcony. Today it is in ruins and a family lives in the back part. According to the nineteenth century local historian Platon Ioseliani there has been a Zoroastrian temple at this site since ancient times. The remains of today date from the seventeenth century. When the Turks controlled the city at the beginning of the eighteenth century (1723-1735) they converted the temple into a mosque. The Islamic components were demolished soon after this period known as *Osmanloba*.

The unmistakable statue of **Mother Georgia** should be almost directly above you at this point. It was designed as a symbol of the nation by Elguja Amashukeli and put up in 1958. The original was

wooden and started to rot after a decade or so. In 1994 the city authorities decided to commission a newer version, the one you see today. It is considered a softer more cuddly version than the original that was much more strident. The cup in her left hand is filled with Georgian wine for friends, but the sword in the right is a warning to enemies.

The tumbledown Belfry on your left dates from the seventeenth century. Next to the Belfry is the **Upper Bethlehem Church** also called the Petkhain Church. This is a particularly unusual church. The original site dates from the founding of the capital in the fifth century. Indeed it is supposed that Sakdukht, the mother of Vakhtang Gorgasali is buried beneath the church. There are stone fragments of the original church to the left of the altar screen. At that time the extent of the building was to the first set of columns that you see today. In the sixteenth century the church was extended up to the second set of columns. The stone work dates from this period. In the seventeenth century both the Upper and Lower Bethlehem churches became Armenian due to the imposition of a heavy taxation policy imposed by the Iranians that the Georgian

Altar, Lower Bethlehem Church

Interior Cupola, Lower Bethlehem Church

Church was unable to pay. The two churches merged into one religious complex called Saint Stephen's Monastery. In 1740 Prince Givi Amilakhvari performed a number of architectural modifications, both extending the church further to its present size and re-fashioning the dome. Frescoes were added of which one remains of God the Father in the dome. The Georgian Church however is planning to remove this and redecorate the interior in the Georgian style. Upper Bethlehem reopened as a Georgian Orthodox church in 1994. During the Soviet period it was used as a toy and cheap jewellery factory.

The end of Gomi Street leads down to the Petkhain Steps. Timothy Beloy, a local Russian architect designed the steps in 1850. His original idea was to cover the staircase with a roof and to have columns abutting from the steps at various junctures. However the full project was never finished. Halfway down the steps on the left is the early eighteenth century **Lower Bethlehem Church**. Originally Armenian, it was built as part of the Saint Stephen's Monastery but became Georgian in the latter part of the eighteenth century. Perhaps the most notable feature is the interior frescoes. They were completed in 1997 and are the work of two young painters David Khidasheli and Merab Chantvikadze. While the scenes from the bible may be familiar there are also various depictions from the history of Georgia. To the left of the entrance door from left to right are depicted King Archil, the Martyr Shushanik, Queen Tamar and Queen Nana and King Mirian. The figures on the wall of the entrance are of David Gareji and Shio Mghvimeli. Saint David of Gareji was one of the thirteenth Syrian fathers who came to Georgia in the sixth century to spread Christianity. The David Gareji complex in Kakheti is certainly a desirable place to visit. Saint Shio was another of the Syrian fathers who came to Georgia in the sixth century. There is a church dedicated to him not far from Mtskheta where he is buried. If you have the opportunity to visit Mtskheta a detour to Shiomgvime Monastery is worth making. On the far wall to the right of the altar rail are Saint Nino the bringer of Christianity to Georgia, Saint Barbara, Saint Ketevan the Martyr and King Demetre I.

The Petkhain Steps lead back down to Lado Asatiani Street. Directly across is Beglar Akospireli Street where the eighteenth century **Moghnin Church** stands. Unfortunately it is in a very poor

Moghnin Church

state and is probably too dangerous to enter. On this site in the Middle Ages stood a Georgian Church dedicated to Saint George. The remains of Moghnin today are Armenian. It is claimed that Saint George's head was buried in the village of Moghnin near Erevan in Armenia. In the eighteenth century part of his skull was moved to this site and hence the name Moghnin was given to the church. In fact there were apparently two churches on this site Large Moghnin and Small Moghnin. It is the large Moghnin that remains. An old disused synagogue is also located near here. This synagogue (3, Anton Catholicos Street) used to be a museum of Georgian Jewish history but has unfortunately closed down. Continue along until the junction of Beglar Akospireli Street and Lermontov Street. Here are some further good examples of the traditional balconies, particularly the blue building, home of the country's main literary journal Literary Georgia. Abesadze Street in the lower corner of the square takes one down back to Leselidze Street. On the right is a rebuilt **Catholic Church**, dedicated to Saint Mary and finished in 1998. When Pope John Paul II visited Georgia in 1999 it was consecrated. Almost next door to the church is the Royal District Theatre. This theatre was only uncovered in 1997.

Old Synagogue

Above - Saint Mary of the Resurrection Catholic Cathedral

Right - Surp Nishan

There are some different claims upon it. Some argue that it was originally a theatre that had fallen into disuse, others that it was a synagogue and yet others that it was one of Lavrenti Beria's many houses in Georgia.

The last church worthy of a visit is **Surp Nishan** dating from the seventeenth century on Akopian Street in a small courtyard. It was built in 1701 on the site of an earlier Georgian church and is distinguishable for its turquoise roof. The church is closed which is unfortunate because there are some interesting frescoes inside. Nevertheless one can appreciate something of the beauty of the church from the outside and there are some fresco remains at the entrance. The memorial to the right of the entrance is of a certain Pirumian who did much to support the church in the nineteenth century.

Back on Baratashvili Street a stroll down to the river and on the opposite bank is a statue of Nikoloz Baratashvili. Some might consider that it bears an uncanny likeness to Pushkin. Indeed little is known of what Baratashvili really looked like and so it seems the sculpture Boris Tsibadze used a degree of artistic licence. The statue was unveiled in 1975. Baratashvili is considered one of the great nineteenth century Georgian poets despite only leaving us with a small collection. The statue shows him holding his collection in his left hand. The surrounding amphitheatre used to host open air renditions of works but is now little used, perhaps mainly because the road junction here is one of the busier ones of the city.

THE CITY CENTRE

RUSTAVELI AVENUE AND MTATSMINDA

Tbilisi's centre is mainly nineteenth and twentieth century. Originally known as Garetubani it was developed in the middle part of the nineteenth century during the period of Georgia's occupation as part of the Russian Empire. A good starting point to explore the centre is Freedom Square. Formerly the square was called Erevan Square. During the Soviet period it had to be named Lenin Square. A statue of the man was pulled down in the euphoric period of Georgia's march to independence in 1990. The building at the south side of the square is **City Hall**. Construction of the building followed a competition announced by the city leaders in 1879. However no design was chosen and instead it was decided to modify the existing building of the police headquarters put up in 1820. Peter Stern, a German architect designed the façades in 1882. In 1886 a clock was installed. The third storey of the building was added between 1910 and 1912 along with the special tower for the clock. City Hall houses both the Mayor of Tbilisi, currently appointed by the president of the country and an elected council called the Tbilisi Sakrebulo. Elections for the mayor are scheduled during 2001.

If you face City Hall the street winding up to the right is called Leonidze and from here one can walk up to see the nineteenth century Armenian and Georgian merchant houses. It is worth stopping to look at the façade of the National Bank at number three Leonidze Street. Leonidze continues as a cobbled street to Paolo Iashvili Street. In the early twentieth century this quarter became the centre for the so-called 'Blue Horn' symbolist movement of poets. Paolo Iashvili lived at number seven. Titsian Tabidze's house museum's is also in the Mtatsminda district at eighteen Griboedov Street.

Iashvili Street runs into Beridze Street at the crossroads with Tchaikovsky Street. The great Russian composer, Petre Tchaikovsky lived at number twelve on the street bearing his name. At those crossroads the first building on the right is where Ilia Chavchavadze published the Iveria newspaper between 1885-1888. At the end of Beridze Street turn left and at the top of the street turn right. A small garden is visible and opposite is the entrance to the **Funicular Railway**. Built in 1905, it is one of the steepest funiculars in the world with an angle of 60 degrees. There are two stops. The summit is the top of Mount Mtatsminda. Mtatsminda is considered a holy mountain and rises to some 400 metres above the Mtkvari River and some 700 metres above sea level. The views of the city are simply spectacular. On clear days one can see the peaks of the Caucasus Mountains to the north. The park was designed during the nineteen thirties but since Georgia's independence has become

very run down. The ruins are of a former restaurant. There are plans to redevelop the area but the cost is considered a little prohibitive at present. For much of the Soviet period it was called Stalin Park and the intrepid or intrigued may be wish to discover a statue of the old dictator in bushes at the end of the fun fair.

Opposite - Looking towards Mtatsminda

Above - City Hall in Freedom Square

Returning down the funicular railway alight at the middle stop to visit the **Church of Saint David**. The original site of Saint David's chapel dates from the early sixth century. David came to Georgia as one of the thirteen Syrian fathers to preach Christianity. He located himself on this mountain at that time uninhabited and slightly away from the town and lived in a cell. Each Thursday he would descend to the city to preach. However the then Persian overlords of the city were fearful of his proselytising and decided to be rid of him. David called upon God for help to continue his works. A miracle is said to have occurred. A pregnant woman of the city was continually ranting against David. God told David the name of her baby's true father while the baby itself was still in its mother's womb. The woman gave birth to a stone. The birth is said to have taken place at the site of what is now Kvashveti Church on Rustaveli Avenue. Kvashveti means 'bore a stone'. As a consequence it came to be believed that those who brought a stone to Saint David would be absolved of sin.

Top - Metalwork design on Baratashvili Street

Right Top - Merchant House in Mtatsminda

Right Bottom - Statue of Sulkhan Saba Orbeliani

The church that stands today dates from 1879 and was built on the original site of Saint David's cell. The interior is completely decorated with frescoes. Surrounding the church is the Pantheon of Writers and Public Figures of Georgia. Here one can find the graves of many of the great poets, writers and influential persons of nineteenth and twentieth century Tbilisi.

The founder of the Georgian romantic school of poetry is buried here, Nikoloz Baratashvili (1817-1845). His is the monument with a harp on top. Influenced by the Russian poets of the period and of translations of Western European literature, his works are imbued with patriotism and nostalgia for Georgia's past. Curiously perhaps he spent much of his brief life in Ganja, but never lost site of his beloved Georgia and particularly Tbilisi. Indeed one of his poems, '*Twilight Over Mtatsminda*' is a eulogy to the place where his body now rests.

'O Mtatsminda! Thou Holy Mount! The sight doth haunt
The soul to thought – a place that wilderness hath wrought
The dew divine like drops of pearl doth grace the sight
And trembling mingles in delight with soft twilight.
Both solitude and silence rule the place in proud and haughty state!
And from that mount my eyes behold a scene that rapture doth create!
Below the plain with ambrosial flowers is like a heavenly altar spread;
The fragrance like the incense sweet its blessing on the Mount doth shed.'

The great Georgian patriot Ilia Chavchavadze (1837-1907) is buried in the central section. His tombstone is in red marble with a depiction of the *Grieving Motherland*. Ilia, now a Saint of the Georgian Orthodox Church, is considered the founder of the Georgian national movement of the nineteenth century. An orphan from a noble Kakhetian family he was sent to Tbilisi to study from age eleven. University education took him to St. Petersburg where he studied law and became profoundly influenced by the new thoughts emanating from Russia's seats of learning. Ilia used his time to write a rich collection of poetry and prose. Rejecting the romanticism of Baratashvili, he attempted to combine notions of national renewal with a sense of civic consciousness. Back in his native Georgia he battled with others to change the nature of the literary language. Chavchavadze believed that the written Georgian language should reflect what people actually said rather than the more elevated courtly and religious style that was normally used. Ilia spent much of his life defending the Georgian language and culture and was instrumental through first his journal *Sakartvelos Moambe* and later *Iveria* in awakening the latent national spirit of the Georgians. It is believed that he was assassinated by the Russian Tsar's police in 1907, because he was considered a danger to imperial rule in the Caucasus.

Ilia's contemporary Akaki Tsereteli (1840-1915) is also buried here. Tsereteli with Chavchavadze was part of the so-called *tergdaleulni* movement (literally those who have drunk the waters of the Terek a river that separates Georgia from Russia). The symbolism was that Georgians should be separate from Russia. Akaki was also concerned with the Georgian national spirit embodied in the countryside and language. He is also famous for his discovery of manganese in the western Georgian town of Chiatura. Ilia and Akaki distinguished themselves from the existing so-called fathers of the Georgian intellectual elite who were happy to work alongside their Russian overlords. These latter were called the *mtkvardaleulni* (those who drank the waters of the Mtkvari river).

A grotto on the lower terrace contains the tombstone of Alexander Griboedov the Russian ambassador and writer. The stone grotto designed by his young sixteen year old widow Nino, the daughter of Alexander Chavchavadze was made in 1832. The sculpture represents a mourning woman kneeling before a cross and bears the inscription: *"your intelligence and deeds will remain immortal in the memory of all Russians but why has my love outlived you."*

Among other notables in the pantheon is Iakob Gogebashvili (1840-1912) the writer of *Deda Ena* the standard school textbook for children to learn Georgian and Vazha Pshavela (1861-1915) considered perhaps the finest of Georgia's nineteenth century romantic poets. Luka Razikashvili, his real name, lived his whole life in the North Eastern province of Georgia Khevsureti, but it was decided to bury him in Tbilisi. His poems are concerned with mountain life. Perhaps his greatest poem is called *The Snake-Eater*.

Other famous Georgians buried here are Kote Marjanishvili (1891-19760, one of the founders of Georgian theatre; the playwright David Eristavi (1847-1890); poet Galaktion Tabidze; sculptor Iakob Nikoladze (1876-1951); the artist Lado Gudiashvili (1896-1980); the novelist Vasil Barnov (1856-1934); the actress Veriko Anjaparidze (1897-1987) and the prominent dissident and nationalist Merab Kostava (1939-1989).

Either the funicular or the path will return you to Chonkadze Street. Any street will eventually return you to Rustaveli Avenue. For those wishing to see where Georgian politicians conduct their business turn right and take the second road down on the left. Chitadze Street takes you past the Ministry of Foreign Affairs on the right. Opposite the ministry is **Saint Nino's Church**, opened and blessed in 1999 to celebrate Georgian independence Day on the 26th May.

Further down on the left is the entrance to the Parliament of Georgia. In the nineteenth century this was the site of one of the main Russian churches in Tbilisi built specifically for the Russian military stationed in Georgia. The current parliament building dates from 1953. It was considerably damaged during the Civil War Tbilisi suffered from in December 1991 and January 1992. Renovated in

Right - Saint David's Church
Opposite - Saint David's
Church Interior

1994 and 1995, it took on the full role of being the country's legislature after parliamentary elections held in November 1995.

The street just before the Parliament on the right Ingorokva Street leads to the Presidential Office normally referred to as the State Chancellery. The gardens were formerly the Palace Gardens of the Russian viceroy. Chitadze Street becomes the Ninth of April Street and takes you to Rustaveli Avenue. Alternatively by visiting the Presidential Office one can go down to the main street by a series of steps. Otherwise the narrow streets of Mtatsminda offer a pleasant

stroll. In Besik Square is a large statue of Sulkhan Saba Orbeliani an important Georgian diplomat and writer from the late seventeenth and early eighteenth century. The Orbeliani family was influential in Georgian life throughout the eighteenth and nineteenth centuries. The family house is now the American Embassy in Tbilisi on Atoneli Street.

Rustaveli Avenue is the main thoroughfare and street of the city. Here Tbilisians perform the Mediterranean custom of the passagiata or paseo. It is the place to see and perhaps more importantly

Right - Saint Nino's Church

Above - Saint Nino's Church interior views

Opposite - Childrens' Palace formerly the Viceroy's Palace

be seen. Georgian drivers also seem to gain an extra thrill when careering down the avenue and as a consequence it is dangerous to cross. There are three underpasses, at Freedom Square, Kvashveti Church and the Opera House.

The creamy white building on the right of Ninth of April Street is called the **Childrens' Palace**. It was built in 1807 as the residence

of the Russian Viceroy in the Caucasus. Designed to conform to the strict Russian classical style of the period it was altered by architect Otto Simonson in 1865 and 1868. Both the façade and much of the interior were changed. Today it is a place for children to use and is open to the public to inspect. In the internal courtyard is the remains of an old sputnik space capsule.

Next to the Freedom Square metro station is an underpass to the other side of the street. The small square adjacent to Freedom Square is called Pushkin Square and has a monument to the great Russian poet and writer, Alexander Pushkin. The city leaders in 1880 decided to commemorate Pushkin's visit to Tbilisi by naming this part of what was Erevan Square after him. The statue is by Felix Khodorovich and dates from 1892. Pushkin himself visited Tbilisi in 1829 and lived at number seven Pushkin Street. Opposite the statue at number one Gudiashvili Street is the State Art Museum. This building was originally the Tbilisi Seminary founded in 1817. The current building, erected by a sugar manufacturer Iakob

Right - Sameba Church
Opposite - The National Library
Opposite - The National Library Interior
Opposite - Statue of Shota Rustaveli
in the National Library

Zubalishvili, dates from 1830 and retains it original features. It became an art gallery in 1952.

The walk up Rustaveli Avenue takes you past the most significant museums and places of entertainment in Tbilisi. The new Arts and Cultural Centre at number three organises both traditional and contemporary exhibitions of Georgian artisans and artists. Also at number three is the imposing building erected in 1929 by Nikolai Severov the Janashia Museum of Georgia. This museum chronicles

the history of the country down to the present. The museum section of this guide provides details.

Purtseladze Street leads to the **National Library of Georgia** at 5 Gudiashvili Street. The main entrance leads to a lovely exhibition room. At the back of the National Library is the **Sameba Church** on Manjgaladze Street. The church was started in 1793 and finished in 1853. It is characteristic of the period but also has a passing nod to Russian classicism. In recent years the church has become popular

for weddings. In the courtyard is one of the main registry offices in Tbilisi. There are two other registry offices - the Soviet built 'Palace of Weddings' and a lovely white balconied house on Baratashvili Street.

The gardens at the end of Gudiashvili Street were designed in honour of Russian Tsar Alexander II. Today they have been renamed the Leonidze Gardens. Where the gardens meet Rustaveli Avenue is the **Kvashveti Church** built between 1904 and 1910 by German architect Leopold Bielfeld. In the grounds of the church is the gravestone of Giorgi Chanturia a prominent nationalist at the time of Georgia's struggle for independence in the late nineteen eighties. He was assassinated in 1994. Kvashveti is unusual in that it is in fact two churches in one building. The upper church is Georgian Orthodox, while the lower church with its entrance to the right facing away from Rustaveli was Russian Orthodox but now appears to be mixed. The design is based upon the Church of Samtavisi located some sixty kilometres northwest of Tbilisi. In the upper church, the altar paintings are by Lado Gudiashvili, composed in 1946. The main door to Kvashveti depicts St. George, to whom the church is

Left - Kvashveti Church

Below - Rustaveli Theatre

National Blue Gallery

dedicated, slaying the dragon. Particularly striking is the stonework of the Agladze brothers on the eastern façade. The oratory in the courtyard was erected in 1897 and contains the grave of a certain Henry Mowatt, a Scottish engineer who assisted in the building of Georgia's first railway linking Western and Eastern Georgia in 1876.

The building with the blue façade at number eleven is called the **National Blue Gallery** and hosts spring and autumn exhibitions. Formerly a museum of military history, it was built in 1885 in a mixture of Renaissance, Classical and Baroque styles. At the other side of Chanturia Street is the unfortunate ruin of Hotel Tbilisi, destroyed during the Civil War of 1991-2. It is currently undergoing extensive renovation under the guidance of the Marriott Hotel chain and Morrison construction company. It is due to open in 2001. On the opposite side of Rustaveli Avenue with the statue of Ilia Chavchavadze and Akaki Tsereteli in the front, is School Number One. Traditionally this has been the place where the city's elite were educated in their formative years. The School dates from 1802 and was called the Tbilisi First Classical Gymnasium. The Russian idea

Paliashvili Opera House

was to produce a yearly crop of highly educated young Georgians to help run the Empire. Schooling was in Russian only but the imperial scheme never really worked as those who studied became some of the most prominent Georgian patriots. The school throughout the Soviet period managed to retain its elite status even if in its curriculum it had to provide a passing nod to the strictures of Marxism and Leninism. The building was extensively damaged in the civil war but was renovated with the help of the Mayor of Moscow and former alumnae. Today it remains by far the best equipped and staffed educational institution in the country.

The **Shota Rustaveli Theatre** is next to Hotel Tbilisi. Built in 1901 by architects Korneli Tatishchev and Alexander Shimkevich, it remains the premier theatre of the city. In addition to the main auditorium that seats 840, there is a smaller theatre as well as classrooms for students of the neighbouring Drama Institute. A basement cafe contains wall paintings of Lado Gudiashvili and David Kakabadze. The Rustaveli Theatre Company was founded in 1921. It is currently under the stewardship of Robert Sturua. Some of the

company's performances particularly of Shakespeare have received critical acclaim in various parts of the world including the performance of Richard III in London's Roundhouse in 1987. Through the difficult years of the early nineteen nineties it is no exaggeration to state that the Rustaveli Theatre kept many spirits alive and helped to keep Georgia's name on the map. During its travels abroad it was able to present an image of Georgia altogether more positive, artistic, and rewarding than the pictures of war and destruction often seen in the Western media during that period.

Again over the road, number sixteen Rustaveli Avenue is the home of the Georgian State Dance Company. If there was one aspect of Georgian culture that was known throughout the world through the Soviet period it was surely the Georgian dancers. Founded in 1945 by Iliko Sukhishvili and Nino Ramishvili through the succeeding years the dance troupe has brought dagger dancing and various examples of folk dances to some eighty seven countries.

Further up Rustaveli is the **Paliashvili Ballet and Opera House**. Zakaria Paliashvili is considered the founder of Georgian opera and

his statue is fittingly in the gardens adjacent to the building. Designed by Merab Berdzenishvili the statue was erected in 1973. Quite often there are performances of his work notably *Daisi* and *Absalom & Eteri*. Tbilisi's first Opera House was built on what is now Freedom Square during the Vorontsov viceroy period in the nineteenth century. In 1870 however it burned down. Architect V.A. Shreter designed this replacement moorish style building in 1880 and work was completed in 1897. In 1973 a fire destroyed all but the front portico and part of the walls of this building. It was rebuilt in 1977 preserving much of the original design, although the interior was considerably modified and extended. During the nineteenth century Verdi's Otello and Tchaikovsky's *Eugine Onegin* were staged here soon after their debuts. Today, particularly in the spring and autumn seasons, the local troop is often joined by members of the *Bolshoi* from Moscow or the *Mariinsky* from St. Petersburg for sometimes dazzling performances.

Across the avenue Alexander Chavchavadze Street leads to the **Sarajishvili Conservatoire** at eight Griboedov Street. Founded in

Above - Statue of Ilia Chavchavadze and Akaki Tsereteli

Left Top - Statue of Nikoloz Baratashvili

Far Left Bottom - Bust of Alexandre Pushkin

Page 80 - Left - Balcony on Sarajishvili Street, Below - Fountain in Pushkin Square, Right - Door front in Mtatsminda

Page 81 - Right - Wedding House on Baratashvili Street, Far Right - House off Lermontov Street, Bottom - Street Light

1917, the conservatoire boasts a number of distinguished students including the bass Paata Burchuladze, the tenor Zurab Shotkilava and pianists Elizo Virsiladze and Lexo Toradze. Further along Griboedov Street at number twenty two is the **Tbilisi Academy of Arts**. The building is one of the finest examples of nineteenth century classical architecture in the city and dates from the late eighteen fifties. In 1902 the left section of the building was reconstructed and the following year it became the home of the Academy of Arts. Here both contemporary and Georgian traditional arts are studied. The second floor has occasional exhibitions of student work.

Opposite the Academy is a flight of stairs that descend to Rustaveli Avenue. In the small alleyway is the Basement Theatre notable for its modern and adventurous productions. As the avenue gently bends, the imposing and some argue in architectural terms confused building of the Academy of Sciences on the corner at number fifty six comes into view. It was built in 1953 during the Soviet period. The spire contains one of the last remaining symbols of the Soviet era – perhaps because nobody can get to the top of it to remove it! The cobbled square at the end of Rustaveli Avenue is called Republican Square, designed in the latter part of the Soviet

era. The concrete arches on the left are normally referred to as *Andropov's Ears*.

Sarajishvili Street to the side of the Academy of Sciences leads up to **Saint Mikheil's Church**. The climb is a little steep. To reach the church take the first lane on the right and continue it round until you see some steps. The steps lead up to the church. Built at the start of the twentieth century between 1904 and 1910 it is a typical example of a Russian Orthodox Church of the period. Today services are held in both Russian and Georgian. Most of the icons in the church are Russian although some of the newer ones are Georgian. In the courtyard of the church and up to the road are some pleasant pines and cypress trees.

Any descent will return you to the centre. Perhaps the most interesting is the following. Some twenty or so metres to the right of the church are some steps. If you take these you can walk down through a number of small neighbourhoods that lead down to Rustaveli Square with its statue of the great Georgian epic writer Shota Rustaveli. The statue is the work of Kote Merabishvili put up in 1937. McDonald's is a very recent addition to the square. With the metro station to your left, walk up Kostava Street until you find the underpass. At the square in front of the Philharmonic Hall turn

Saint Mikheil's Church

right on Nikoladze Street. At the end of this street on the left are two churches tucked away in their own courtyard. The white coloured church is Russian Orthodox dedicated to Ivan Bogoslov. It was built in 1901 under the direction of the Russian viceroy of the period Prince Golitsyn.

Next to it is the **Blue Monastery** (*lurdji monasteri*) that dates from Queen Tamar's period in the twelfth century. The name

Statue of Shota Rustaveli

derives from the turquoise tiles that once adorned the roof. The current blue is recent. The church is an elongated rectangle in design. The dome rests upon the jutting walls of the apse and two free standing octahedral pillars. During the seventeenth and eighteenth centuries the monastery underwent extensive modification. The parts surviving from the twelfth century are the dressed stonework of the lower walls and the windows with surrounding

85

Opposite Page - The Blue Monastery
Right - Ivan Bogoslov Church

ornamentation. The interior has three naves and is simple in form and design. The inscription on the southern facade relates that the church was built in dedication to Saint Andrew by Archbishop Basil of Kartli. The courtyard leads through to Vera Park. During the summer months a number of cafes open up. Close by one can sample one of the many bars and restaurants on what has become Tbilisi's main restaurant district, Akhvlediani Street normally known by its older name of Perovskaya.

OUTSIDE THE CENTRE

DIDUBE AND THE LEFT BANK

On the left or north bank of the river stretches the Didube region of Tbilisi a sprawling region of low rise apartment blocks. There are two main arteries on this side of the river, Aghmashenebeli Avenue and Tsereteli Avenue. Aghmashenebeli Avenue was called Michael Street during the nineteenth century and in Soviet times Plekhanov Avenue. The region started to develop in the eighteen thirties when Aghmashenebeli then called Mikhailovskaya Street linked up the villages of Kukia, Chughureti and Didube. As the nineteenth century turned to the twentieth so the left bank began to rival the centre as a city focal point. However it was really during the Soviet period that Tsereteli Avenue and its surrounds developed and most of the buildings date from the mid twentieth century. Less picturesque perhaps than the centre and old town, there are nevertheless some interesting sights.

At number fifty four Aghmashenebeli Avenue is the house where Leo Tolstoy stayed between 1851 and 1852. The square half way along the avenue is Marjanishvili Square a bustling shopping area. Just off the southwest corner of the square on Marjanishvili Street leading to the river is the Marjanishvili Theatre. Its founder Kote Marjanishvili established the theatre in Kutaisi in Western Georgia in 1928 before moving it to Tbilisi. Today the theatre's main impresario is Keti Dolidze, one of the doyen's of Tbilisi's artistic circles. Keti arranges an annual festival called the Gift Festival – a celebration of drama and the arts normally held in September and October.

Up from Marjanishvili Square on Ivane Javakhishvili Street is a Russian Orthodox Church dedicated to Alexander Nevsky at number sixty five. It was built in the eighteen nineties. Further down Javakhishvili Street is the Saint Peter and Paul Catholic church. The church was built between 1870 and 1877, from a design by Albert Zaltsman, a local Tbilisi architect. Catholic missionaries came to Georgia in the eighteenth and nineteenth centuries mainly in the south of the country. Daily mass is at 9.00am and on Sundays at the same time in English.

Back on Aghmashenebeli Avenue, the city's main concert hall is at number one hundred and twenty three. Queen Tamar Avenue crosses Aghmashenebeli and just over the other side on the left behind a small garden is the Tumanishvili Theatre – a modern construction. In the garden is a statue of the late Mikheil Tumanishvili. Performances of his rendition of Shakespeare's Midsummer Nights Dream are utterly unforgettable. Next door to the theatre is the German Embassy in a building lovingly restored to its former glory. It is no accident why the German Embassy is located here as this area was a main German quarter of the city during the nineteenth

Alexander Nevsky Russian Church

century. Germans first came to Tbilisi in the early part of the nineteenth century. Soon after their arrival in 1820 they built a little
wooden church. In 1892 architect Leopold Bielfeld designed a new
Lutheran church. However it was closed during the Second World
War. In the middle of the nineteen nineties it was decided to build a
brand new church and this is situated on Terenti Graneli Street not
far from the statue of Maxim Gorky.

Peter and Paul Catholic Church

The next major landmark is the Paichadze National Stadium home of Dynamo Tbilisi. The stadium is due to undergo some changes to conform to UEFA safety standards but has a capacity currently of some 80,000. Unfortunately the glory days of Dynamo Tbilisi are in the past. Football is a passion in Tbilisi and rivals other football crazy cities. Dynamo Tbilisi still tries to nourish the undoubted talents of aspiring football players but it has difficulty

Didube Church

finding good opposition. Thus many young Georgian stars now grace the football fields of Britain, Holland and Germany.

To the north of the stadium is the central market of the city and the famous flea market or *bazroba* (see the practical information section for details). To the east of the market is the main railway station for all inter-city routes and for trains to Azerbaijan. Rail links to Armenia are from the other railway station in Krtsanisi.

From the railway station it is possible to take the number 130 microbus to Tbilisi Sea. This is actually a reservoir based upon a natural depression but enlarged in 1951. Fed by the Iori River the purpose of the reservoir is to serve the arid lands of the Samgori steppe to the east. For many years Tbilisi Sea has been a favourite swimming spot for Tbilisians.

Moving along Tsereteli Avenue on the left just past the metro station is the Church of the Didube Virgin. The original church dating from Queen Tamar's time in the twelfth century was destroyed during the Mongol invasions. The current church was built between 1874 and 1884 from funds collected by local residents of Didube. While it is not the most remarkable of the city's churches, there are some interesting nineteenth century frescoes. Today the church, while serving the local community, also houses the second pantheon in the city for famous Georgian luminaries and writers. One of the most notable is the tombstone of the artist Elene Akhvlediani.

Tsereteli Avenue stretches further to the west and links to the western suburb of Dighomi where Tbilisi's main film studios are located at 6 Akhmeteli Street. Georgian film was particularly renowned in the Soviet times and was perhaps more daring in its approach than those in other republics. Directors such as Tengiz Abuladze, Revaz Chkheidze, Otar Ioselliani and the Shengelaia brothers all worked here.

Dighomi suburb leads to the undistinguished suburbs of Gldani, Mukhiani and Temka. Marshall Gelovani Avenue is the main artery for leaving the city for the West of the country including the ancient capital Mtskheta and also links to the Georgian Military Highway for Ananuri, Kazbegi and the Russian border.

VAKE

Chavchavadze Avenue and Paliashvili Street are the main thoroughfares of the Vake district. Before the twentieth century this area was uninhabited. However the decision to place the country's main university at the junction of Chavchavadze Avenue and Varazis-Khevi Street undoubtedly assisted the process of general construction. Tbilisi State University was founded during Georgia's period of independence in the early twentieth century. In the grounds of the main building there is now a small chapel as well as busts of the founders and greats of Tbilisi's academic world. Recent years have not been kind to the university. Many private institutions some not of the highest quality have sprung up and the brightest students now look to study abroad to increase their knowledge and skills. Nevertheless in some fields – more particularly in the pure sciences Tbilisi State University still distinguishes itself.

Many of the buildings stretching up Chavchavadze Avenue belong to the university. In the university's eighth building at number thirteen is the home of the British Council in Georgia. The adjoining streets are considered some of the most prestigious in the city and at least up until independence housed many of the academics and writers of the city. Economic hardship however has somewhat reduced the region although it is still considered a good place to live by many foreigners who come to work in Tbilisi.

Halfway up the avenue on the right is a park for children called the Mziuri Park, designed by the novelist Nodar Dumbadze. Dumbadze himself is buried in the grounds near the entrance. The park follows the contours of the Vera River valley and has some unusual sculptures and statues.

At the top of Chavchavadze Avenue on the left is Vake Park - a huge expanse covering some 226 hectares that stretches up the Trialeti Ridge. In the summer months the main waterfall sometimes works. Through Vake Park one can reach the Ethnographic Museum as well as Turtle Lake.

SABURTALO

Saburtalo is a large sprawling suburb built around Gamsakhurdia Avenue, Vazha Pshavela Avenue and the continuation from the centre of town of Kostava Avenue. The increased demands for housing in the nineteen sixties led to the development of the suburb and much of what one sees is the eight by sixteen Soviet tenement blocks. Tucked behind the main streets are some more pleasant single and double storey dwellings. Saburtalo begins at Heroes Square – one of the city's main intersections – and incredibly dangerous to drive around. Both the city zoo and circus are situated here. The zoo has suffered more than other city attractions over the last ten years but is worth a short visit. The main state television studios are just up the road from the zoo at number sixty eight Kostava Street.

Lisi Lake at Saburtalo's North West extent is a quiet and tranquil spot. The lake is at the end of Ossetian Street. You will need a taxi to reach it, as public transport is less than regular.

In the heart of Saburtalo is the Adjara Hotel, a large Soviet era complex now full of refugees. Adjacent to it is the Sports Palace, where primarily basketball is played. It also doubles as one of the main rock and pop venues in the city particularly for more famous bands. For horse racing fans there is a track called the Hippodrome. The entrance is at 13 Tamarashvili Street, the road connecting Saburtalo to Vake. Devotees of modern architecture may want to check the building of the highways department on Gagarin Street where the street descends towards the Right Bank.

AVLABARI AND ISANI

Avlabari district is the main district for Tbilisi's Armenian community. It stretches from Baratashvili Rise through Ketevan the Martyr Avenue. At the junction with the Sheraton Metechi Hotel the district of Isani begins and this stretches to the outskirts of town. For many these districts are the first to be seen upon entering the

Akhvlediani Rise

city. This is because this is the principal route from the Tbilisi Airport and for departure to the eastern Georgian region of Kakheti. There are no particular sites to view here as the districts are essentially residential.

ORTACHALA AND KRTSANISI

These are the districts of the city that lead to routes for Rustavi, and for those driving to Armenia. Ortachala essentially starts at Gorgasali Square close to the Sulphur Baths. Some 200 metres from the baths moving eastwards is a former Greek Orthodox church dedicated to Tsar Nicholas I. It was built in 1876. While the church is now Georgian there are still some interesting frescoes of Greek origin. Tbilisi has for a long period been home to a small Greek community that is based in this quarter of the city.

Krtsanisi is the district of the President's residence. Not open to the public and normally heavily guarded, Krtsanisi is built around the brow of the hill. Within the complex there are a number of dachas. The Organisation for Security and Cooperation in Europe's Georgian headquarters is based here and this is also where the country's distinguished guests would normally reside. Often government conferences and functions are held here.

CHUGHURETI

Chughureti is a small district linking Avlabari to Didube on the northern bank of the river. The European Commission has its delegation headquarters here on Nino Chkheidze Street. The building is in a distinctive mustard yellow colour. Upon the same street as the European Commission is the eighteenth century Saint Nino's church. Just above the statue of Nikoloz Baratashvili near Akhvlediani Rise is the church of All Mtatsminda dating from the nineteenth century. By the river bank on Khetagurov Street is the early nineteenth century church of Saint Nicholas. Inside there are some very good frescoes painted by Gigo Zaziashvili. Further along the embankment past Saarbruken Square just off Uznadze Street is a statue to Alexander Griboedov. The statue was designed by Merab Merabishvili in 1961.

Lermontov Street

MUSEUMS AND GALLERIES

Tbilisi is blessed with a number of fine museums that allow further exploration of various aspects of the country's history and culture. The following section describes the contents of the main museums and gives the addresses of the more specialist ones devoted to a particular writer or artist. As a general rule museums do not open much before midday and are closed on Sundays and Mondays. If you find an area of specific interest the bibliography at the end of the book should point you to more detailed investigation.

The curators of the various museums are particularly keen to forge links with the outside world. The majority of the collections were set up during the Soviet period when there were large subsidies for art and culture. Georgian independence has brought hard times. With few state subsidies and in the last few years only a trickle of visitors, the museums face difficult futures. That said there are many rich treasures to view. In most museums photography is not allowed but you can get special permission in exceptional cases. We plan in the future to produce a separate volume on the city's museums but for now the following pages should prove a useful introduction.

JANASHIA MUSEUM OF GEORGIA
3 Rustaveli Avenue Tel. 997176.
Tuesday – Sunday 11.00 – 16.00. Admittance 50 tetris, for the treasury there is an additional charge of three dollars

The Janashia is the main museum in Georgia and covers the history of the country from prehistoric times up to the turn of the twentieth century. The mediaeval collection is closed at present and perhaps not surprisingly so is the twentieth century collection. Particularly significant is the treasury in the basement where one must be accompanied by a guide.

The ground floor provides a history of the country up to the fourth century BC. The first room on the left of the entrance shows artefacts up to 10,000 BC – stone implements from the Acheuleana and Mousterian periods, found in Eastern and Western Georgia. Noteworthy are the shell necklace, alabaster pendants, pierced bone ornaments and a fragment of a staff. In the second room we move to the sixth to fourth millennia BC with bronze tools and weapons and pottery (*cases 17-19*), altar stones, terracotta statues, and pots decorated with deer (*case 20*). There are also bronze and silver weapons, decorated items made from melted wax and silver vessels with hunting motifs (*cases 21-25*). Case 24 contains bronze axes and agricultural implements from Ureki. In front of case 24 is the funeral chariot of a tribal chief dating from the twentieth century BC.

*Top - Tondo of Saint Mamai
Riding a Lion*

*Above - Golden Goblet of King
Bagrat III and Queen
Gurandukht*

Back across the entrance hall room three covers the Late Bronze Age (14th century BC) to the Early Iron Age (13th century BC). Here you can see cast metal works found near Tskhinvali, weapons, bronze and iron artefacts, ceramics some of which are glazed and an early potter's wheel. Also there are early forms of money in bronze and iron.

The adjoining room four is dedicated to the Iron Age (14th century to 4th century BC). Cases 34-37 contain weapons, a horse harness, jewellery, and pre-Christian religious objects from burial sites. Extensive archaeological research was performed at Khovlegora and on the wall is a plan of the site. In the centre of the room is a scaled cross section of one of the remains there. On the far wall is a map detailing the archaeological finds in Georgia. The map is colour coded. Black refers to the Upper Palaeolithic, Red – Lower Palaeolithic, Gold – Neolithic, Orange – Eneolithic, Blue – Early Bronze Age, Brown – Middle Bronze Age, Green – Late Bronze Age, White – Antique Era.

This room also contains artefacts from the kingdoms of Colchis and Iberia. Case 38 shows sixth century BC silver coins from Colchis, gold and silver jewellery and goblets from burial sites. In cases 39-44 there are fertility rite figurines, beads, amber and glass-ware. There are also examples here of early metal chasing, enamel-work, as well as bone and wood carving. Archaeological research in the old capital Mtskheta in 1867 uncovered monuments with epigraphs. One of them shown here describes the reinforcement of walls of a fortress by the Roman Emperor Vespasian. The inscription reads *"To King Mithridate of Iberia – Friend of Caesar and of the Romans"*.

Taking the stairs back at the entrance to the first floor one swiftly moves to the nineteenth century. The collection covers the period when Georgia was part of the Russian Empire. The accompanying explanations are still written in 'Soviet Speak'. Room one shows the guns, sabre and gunpowder flask of Erekle II and the gun of King Solomon II of Kakheti as well as the portraits of Georgian generals who fought in the Russian-Turkish war of 1812.

The second room displays various aspects of life in nineteenth century Georgia, from artisan tools to the first Georgian newspapers and periodicals. Also there are examples of the development of the arts and music.

On the museum's top floor is a curious yet pleasant ethnographic room. Here you can see Georgian musical instruments, nineteenth century rural and city style costumes. There are also two replica houses showing something of how people lived two hundred or so years ago. One house is rural while the other would have been for a city gentleman.

Top - Eleventh century enamel

Above - Tenth century enamel from Chemokmedi

Opposite - Three medallion enamels from Tsalenjika, twelfth century

If you look out on the veranda at the back of the museum there is a large glassed case in the courtyard. This contains the skeleton of an elephant, some 4.5 metres tall found in Kakheti in 1950. Apparently there are few such examples in the world.

Before leaving, the treasury in the museum's basement is well worth visiting. The first case in the collection contains gold work from Kakheti from the early Bronze Age, including a tiny golden lion dating from 2,600 BC. The second case has jewellery from Trialeti from the same period and includes a golden bowl encrusted with precious stones dating from roughly 1,800 BC., a silver cup with depictions of hunting and religious rituals and a king's sceptre. Archaeological finds from Vani in Western Georgia dominate the third case. Here there are earrings and necklaces including one with thirty one tiny turtles and a splendid diadem. These artefacts date from the fifth century BC. The fourth case has finely granulated necklaces and bracelets and an enamelled pendant. In the fifth case are finds from the Racha region of the country; bracelets, signet rings and coins again from the fifth century BC. The final cases numbers six and seven from the same period reveal discoveries made in the Eastern part of the country. Here there are golden buckles, silver earrings, sheep's head rings, a necklace of frogs and a delightful pair of golden pendants with depictions of horses with a harness.

The eighth case of the collection takes us forward to the 2nd century AD and finds from the old capital of Georgia, Mtskheta. Here there is a cornelian and gold signet of Asparuch and a sheath for a dagger. The next case, number nine, shows jewellery from a queen's tomb, including a ring of gold and amethyst depicting the death of Actaeon, a diadem of garnet and gold as well as silver bowls from Greece. The following case has agate scent bottles and a necklace with an amethyst sheep's head that contains two teeth of the daughter of the queen mentioned above.

In the eleventh case we move onwards to the third century when encrustation took over from granulation and gold served mainly as a support for precious stones. In the twelfth case there is a king's funeral crown with golden oak leaves set with garnet and pearls. The thirteenth case has more gold leaves as well as rings, bracelets, coins and a dolphin set in gold and carved in agate. By the fourteenth case we have moved on one more century and here there is a bowl decorated with grape and wine motifs as well as earrings and bracelets of garnet and jet. The final case has artefacts from the mountain region of Svaneti including a pin of agate and gold, buckles with cornelian and a gold house with two musicians and birds on the roof.

*Fifteenth century enamel
of Saint George and the Dragon*

GEORGIAN ART MUSEUM

1 Gudiashvili Street Tel. 996635.
Tuesday – Sunday 11.00 – 16.00. Admittance 50 tetris, for the treasury there is an additional charge of three dollars

This is Tbilisi's main gallery and provides a useful introduction to Georgian painting, particularly of the nineteenth and twentieth century. Today parts of the collection are in storage for security reasons and the basement treasury is sometimes closed. However if you do find it open, the treasury is an absolute must to visit. Here you can find some of Georgia's most exquisite and prized possessions both royal and ecclesiastical.

Twelfth century Khakhuli icon

The main piece of the collection is the *Kakhuli Triptych*. The triptych was made in the twelfth century to frame a cloisonné icon of the Virgin that dates from the tenth century. The icon hails from the Kakhuli Monastery now in Turkey. During the period of David the Builder the icon was transferred to the Gelati monastery in Western Georgia where the triptych was added. The setting is embossed gold while the side pieces are gilded silver typical of tenth century Georgian design. All that remains of the central part are the hands and face of the Virgin.

Queen Tamar's Cross is a golden pectoral cross dating from the twelfth century. It is studded with four emeralds, six pearls and five rubies.

Above - Pirosmani, Woman with an Umbrella

Right - Elene Akhvlediani, Old Tbilisi 1938.

Opposite - David Kakabadze, Landscape

Opposite - Pirosmani, Fisherman

The Icon of the Saviour of Anchi is the oldest example of Georgian icon painting and dates from the sixth century. The embossed gold setting was added in the twelfth century and is the work of Beka Opizari a celebrated Georgian goldsmith. It was brought to Tbilisi in the seventeenth century when the monastery of Anchi in Tao fell into Turkish hands.

The Gold Goblet of King Bagrat III and Queen Gurandukht was made in 999 from a single piece of gold and is embossed with the figures of Christ, the Virgin and ten saints. *The Tondo of Saint Mamai Riding a Lion* is an eleventh century silver plaque.

The first floor of the museum houses collections of European and Russian artists as well as reproductions of various Georgian monuments. Included among the western art is a seventeenth century portrait of a senator of the Contarini family by a contemporary of Titian, a Winterhalter portrait of a lady from 1855 and a Kandinsky abstract from 1911. Among the Russian paintings and artefacts are icons from Moscow and Yaroslav dating from the sixteenth century and then a number of at least for western eyes rather unknown Russian painters, including SF Shedrin (1791-1830), Ilia E Repin (1844-1930), Valentin A Serov (1865-1911) and the Tbilisian Grigory Gagarin (1810-1893). On the ground floor to the right of the door is a small oriental collection containing sixteenth to nineteenth century Persian miniatures and carpets.

The collections finally come into their own on the top floor, representing the early twentieth century, when Georgian art reinvented a richly layered voice of its own. Here we can see the

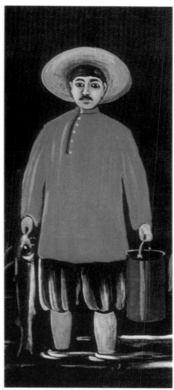

inspired lyrical paintings by Lado Gudiashvili (1896-1980) , important city scapes of Paris and Tbilisi by Elene Akhvlediani (1901-1976), and the modernist works of David Kakabadze (1889-1952), Georgia's first cubist. However particular note must be made of Pirosmani (Niko Pirosmanashvili), 1862-1918. Pirosmani has often been compared with Henri Rousseau as he was self-taught and like him he became a mascot for more sophisticated artists of the period. He was 'discovered' in 1912 by the Russian futurists and the following year exhibited with them in Moscow. He died in penury and virtual obscurity in Tbilisi about five years later. However, since his death, his legend has grown. His paintings (oil paint on black oil cloth) have a monumental quality even when small. Favourite subjects are feasting and still life. In the latter he celebrates the unique qualities of Georgian cuisine; in the former, the rituals of Georgian comradeship and hospitality. Pirosmani remains the essential artist for Tbilisians in particular and Georgians more broadly.

Should you wish to delve further into the lives and works of Georgian artists there are a number of specialist house museums. Normally located in a house or apartment where the painter lived they present details of their life and works. Today most of these small museums are run by relations of the family and have somewhat erratic opening hours. If you do express an interest they may well open especially for you. Of the house museums the one devoted to the life and works of Elene Akhvlediani is perhaps the most attractive, described by one traveller as designed 'to suggest that she will be returning at any moment'. In the centre of the museum is a wooden column modeled on rural architecture and her paintings can be seen stretching up most of the walls. There are also photographs and mementos as well as some of her illustrations for books, films and theatre designs.

Elene Akhvlediani – 12 Kiacheli Street, Tel. 997412. **Pirosmani** – 29 Pirosmani Street Tel. 958673. **Mose Toidze** – 1-3 Tsulukidze Street Tel. 990149

GEORGIAN LITERARY MUSEUM

8 Chanturia Street Tel. 998667
Tuesday – Sunday 11.00 – 17.00. Admittance free

Given that Georgian has its own script and the language is extremely difficult its literature may appear a little impenetrable. Fortunately though there are a number of translations of the major works. The literary museum is more of a research centre and repository for nineteenth and early twentieth century Georgian literature and the personal effects of writers than a traditional museum. Within the museum on the ground floor is the Hobi Gallery that has temporary exhibitions of contemporary artists. The gallery is entered through a room designed as a late nineteenth century salon. The upper floors house the museum itself. The curator's idea is to present selections from the extensive archives. Thus exhibits tend to be on display for two months before being replaced. However those with a particular interest in a certain author or period may request material. A computerised catalogue is being produced that should be completed by the end of 2000. For British readers, it may be interesting to know that there is a collection of

The Silk Museum

the works, letters and some personal memorabilia of Marjory and Oliver Wardrop. Oliver was the first British Consul in Georgia between 1918-1921. Both he and his sister Marjory fell much in love with the Georgians. Marjory Wardrop was the first person to translate Shota Rustaveli's *The Knight in the Panther Skin* into English as well as collections of Georgian poetry. Oliver wrote a book on Georgia with the delicious title *The Kingdom of Georgia -The Land of Wine, Women and Song.*

There are a number of specialist house museums. As with the house museums of artists these tend to be family run and normally closed. It is hence better to ring in advance to see whether the museum will open.

Nikoloz Baratashvili – 17 Chakhrukhadze Street, Tel. 990699. **Ilia Chavchavadze** – 7 Javakhishvili Street, Tel. 957268. **Titsian Tabidze** – 18 Griboedov Street Tel. 999733

TBILISI HISTORY MUSEUM

The Caravansarai, 8 Sioni Street Tel. 982281, 721706
Tuesday – Saturday 11.00 – 16.00. Admittance 50 tetris

The introduction of this volume provides an overview of the city's history and in this museum you can see photographs, paintings and artefacts that illustrate it. The museum is particularly strong on nineteenth century Tbilisi. The main collection is on the ground floor of one of Tbilisi's surviving Caravansarai. The upper floors house temporary exhibitions of modern artists. The starting point is at the left hand door as you enter the museum. The first artefacts are from the Mtkvari-Araks culture found in the Avlabari district of the city, dating from the twenty-fifth to twenty-third centuries BC. Swiftly one moves on to the early mediaeval era with maps locating Tbilisi and a picture of the city's founder Vakhtang Gorgasali. There are a few cases with portraits of kings from the mediaeval period as well as Vakhushti Bagrationi's specialist map of the city from 1735.

The remaining parts of the museum show aspects of life during the nineteenth century and are mostly labelled in English. Also there is a detailed model of the Metechi Palace compound now destroyed. On the walls are a number of interesting photographs from the nineteenth and early twentieth centuries showing churches now no longer in existence and other buildings from that period. There are also reproductions of artisan workshops, a wine cellar and residential houses. There is also an engraving of Alexandre Dumas and for British visitors photographs of Oliver and Marjory Wardrop in Georgian national costumes. The museum abruptly halts at the time of Georgia's period of independence between 1918 and 1921, indeed there is little mention of it. Presumably there must be plans somewhere to bring matters up to date.

The Gelati Gospels, twelfth century

ETHNOGRAPHIC MUSEUM

74 Chavchavadze Avenue Tel. 230960
Tuesday – Saturday 11.00 – 16.00. Admittance 4 lari

On a hillside at the edge of the city in the Vake district through Vake Park, the Ethnographic Museum presents houses and dwellings from all the different regions of the country. The museum was the brainchild of Longinoz Sumbadze a professor of architecture in Georgia and opened in 1968. It has been well preserved despite the instability in the country during the early nineteen nineties and is well worth a visit. Rather than build models of the varying types of dwelling throughout the country, each house was taken down from its original spot and rebuilt in the museum. Today you will find that a number of artisans work in the houses maintaining a particular region's craftsmanship.

The museum covers some 45 hectares so it may be that more than one visit is required to see everything. Divided into ten zones the exhibits are organised according to the regional make-up of the country. The Colchis Zone shows examples of dwelling houses and farmsteads from Guria and Mingrelia regions in the west of the country. If you move round in the museum in a clockwise direction, i.e., left from the entrance the first house you should see a large open-plan house called an *oda-sakhli* from Abasha in Mingrelia. Next is a farmstead also from Mingrelia with a chimney. There are then two houses from Guria both dating from the middle of the nineteenth century. In the Western Zone there is an eighteenth century wooden house called a *sajalabo* from Imeretia made of logs on a stone base. This is followed by three further farmsteads all nineteenth century. This zone concludes with a farm house from the Racha region of the country called a *shua sakhli*. At the top of the museum is a Svanetian tower brought from the regional centre of Mestia. From the mountains we move to the eastern region of Kakheti and a mid-nineteenth century *darbazi* type house brought from the village of Giorgitsminda. There is then a seventeenth century darbazi from the village of Chachlari near the cave city of Vardzia in the south of the country. Representing the Kartli or central region of Georgia is a *darbazi* type dwelling from Karagaji and a flat-roofed *baniani-sakhli* house from Upper Khandaki that also has an area for making wine called a *marani*. The final part of the museum has examples of Georgian historical monuments including the sixth century basilica of Tianeti Sioni – taken from its original spot when the area was made into a reservoir. There is also a sarcophagus from Balichi that dates from the sixth-seventh centuries and contains an ancient Georgian inscription.

SILK MUSEUM

6 Tsabadze Street Tel. 347850
Tuesday – Saturday 11.00 – 16.00. Admission Free

Alavardi Gospels, 1054

Tbilisi's Silk Museum is believed to be the only museum of its type in Europe. Located on the second floor, door immediately at the top of the stairs, the museum traces both the history of silk in Georgia as well as the complete production process from the mulberry bush to the completed article. The museum was created by Nicholas Shavrov (1858-1915), a local Russian from Tbilisi. Shavrov travelled to Western Europe during 1885-87 to study silk production and on his return set about establishing the silk museum. His vision was completed in 1893 and has always been at its present site. For a number of years including during the Soviet period, the museum played an important role in the production of silkworms and the development of sericulture in the Caucasus and Russia.

Divided into two rooms with an adjoining library the visit should start at the far room on the right. This room displays the start of the process of producing silk. There are samples of mulberry trees some over one hundred years old. On the right hand wall are folk musical instruments made from mulberry. The cases display pests collected by Shavrov.

In the main room there are models of incubators and cases of silk worms dating from the late nineteenth and early twentieth centuries. There is also a grass snake – the protector of the mulberry bush. Also there are examples of feeding silkworms and transportation boxes. The museum has some 5000 different silkworm species and cocoons collected not only from Georgia but also Europe, India and Japan. Unfortunately a unique collection of silkworm butterflies was almost totally destroyed during the museum's temporary closure in the latter part of the Soviet period. Nevertheless one or two examples survived. Indeed there was a period when it was believed the museum would be completely dismantled. Fortunately it has survived although it requires some form of financial support if it is to continue over the coming decade. One hopes this will be forthcoming.

The collection finishes with a large display of different silks from different parts of the world. Perhaps, though the most interesting are the examples of Georgian silk production from the nineteenth century. On display are belts and handkerchiefs and striped woven silk in the distinctive Caucasian style used as wall hangings.

The library contains material in some fourteen languages dating from the seventeenth century onwards. Of particular note is a Chinese drawing on rice paper detailing silk production.

FOLK AND APPLIED ART

Sololaki Ridge, by the statue of Mother Georgia
Tuesday – Friday 11.00 to 17.00. Admittance Fifty Tetris

The museum is difficult to reach and so the following may help. Essentially the museum is beneath the statue of Mother Georgia on the Sololaki Ridge. That said there are three ways of reaching it. If you have visited Narikala as you leave the main entrance there is a path to your left. The walk to the museum is about fifteenth minutes and if you keep to the path you cannot miss it. The second method is to take a very steep path from the Upper Bethlehem Church – you will need to be a reasonable climber and in the spring and summer beware of snakes! Winding up through bushes and trees after around ten minutes you should reach the summit. The final part is a series of steps leads directly to the museum. The third way that can also be negotiated by car, although walking is better, is from the Sololaki district. Microbus number 12 winds up through the narrow street of the district. Stop the bus some one hundred metres after it turns into Davitashvili/Amaghleba Street. On the left is a turning and this is the start of a half hour walk that takes you up to Mother Georgia and the museum. The turning is called Amaghleba Rise.

Following all these different ways to reach the museum is it worth it? Yes. The museum has three rooms packed with various examples of Georgian handicraft and folk art and costumes from different parts of the country, all mainly dating from the nineteenth and early twentieth century. There are carpets, Khevsuretian and other mountain garments, musical instruments, tapestries, wooden, ceramic and silver cups, goblets and vases, antique daggers and jewellery and a host of other artefacts. Also there are small models showing carpet making and wine making amongst others. Most of the collection is described in English and perhaps one day there will be a separate small guide explaining all the different artefacts. The museum dates from 1899, although it has only recently been at its current location.

INSTITUTE OF MANUSCRIPTS

3rd building, 1 Merab Alexidze Street Tel. 334708, 332454
By appointment only. Admittance free

While the Institute of Manuscripts is not a museum as such, if you can gain access it is well worth visiting to see something of the rich legacy of illuminated manuscripts housed here. Altogether the institute has some ten thousand works the earliest of which are palimpsests from the fifth century. Of particular interest are the *Alaverdi Four Gospels* dating from 1054, the *Lailashi Bible* written in Hebrew from the tenth century, the twelfth century *Gelati Gospels* and *the Homilies* of Gregory Nazianzus. The institute also has early versions of Shota Rustaveli's *The Knight in the Panther Skin*, and a whole treasure trove of Georgian works.

However the collection is not exclusively Georgian as there are also important works in Amharic, Arabic, Armenian, Greek, Hebrew, Persian, Syriac, Ottoman and Turkish, as well as Russian and Old Church Slavonic. Currently there are plans to improve the condition of where the manuscripts are kept as well as the construction of new reading rooms and the possibility of a permanent exhibition space.

MERAB KOSTAVA MEMORIAL MUSEUM

1 Zandukeli Street, Tel. 988598
Tuesday – Friday 11.00 to 17.00. Admittance Fifty Tetris

Those with a political interest in the country will wish to visit this small museum dedicated to the life of nationalist and dissident Merab Kostava. The museum is in a small courtyard above Rustaveli Square – a little building with a white fence in the far left corner of the yard. Merab Kostava along with Georgia's first president Zviad Gamsakhurdia formed the Helsinki Watch Committee in Tbilisi in 1977, but was later arrested for nationalist activity and exiled to Siberia. Released in 1987 he was part of the developing nationalist movement in Georgia. He died in mysterious circumstances in a car accident in 1989, never to see his cherished ambition of Georgia as an independent country. A political party was set up under his name that in the immediate aftermath of independence and enjoyed a fair measure of support.

GALLERIES

There are a number of art galleries and centres that host temporary exhibitions of predominantly but not exclusively Georgian art and culture. *Tbilisi Pastimes* and *Georgia Today* both provide weekly listings. The galleries are:

Blue National Gallery *11 Rustaveli Avenue*, Carvasla *Caravansarai 8 Sioni Street*, Chardin Gallery *12 Chardin Street*, Georgian Arts and Cultural Centre *3 Rustaveli Avenue*, Hobby Gallery *8 Chanturia Street*, La Maison Bleue Art Studio *28 Gogebashvili Street*, Modern Art Gallery *3 Rustaveli Avenue*, N Gallery *17a Shavteli Street*, Old Gallery *21 Erekle II Street*, Orient Gallery *10 Chardin Street*, TMS Gallery *16 Rustaveli Avenue*, Vernissage Gallery *Beneath Republican Square*.

Sport Hotel Gudauri

is an international standard hotel located 2000 metres above sea level on the southern slopes of the Cauca
Mountains. All the rooms have en suite facilities. The hotel also has a swimming pool, indoor tennis cou
bowling lanes, saunas and whirlpool.

In winter Gudauri is the prefect location for skiers from beginners to experts alike and there is
snowboarding, and heli-skiing. The ski season lasts from December until the end of April.

In summer there are many opportunities to enjoy the splendours of the Caucasus Mountains. We have a spe
helicopter trip to a volcanic plateau with many volcanic lakes, including a short stop at a glacier above 40
metres and a tour around Mount Kazbeg. The hotel also offers horse riding, hiking trips and moun
river fishing.

Sport Hotel Gudauri is also a perfect location for conferences, workshops and meetings.

Tel +995 32 001162, +995 99 559222/579222 Fax +995 32 001163
Email hotel@gudauri.ge or gudauri@access.sanet.ge - www.georgia.net.ge/gudauri

CUISINE

One of the sheer joys of Tbilisi is sampling Georgian cuisine and the splendid locally produced wines. The table is where many of the distinctive qualities of Georgian custom in the form of friendship, hospitality and culture are revealed. It is more than likely that, however brief one's visit to Tbilisi, you will be invited to what is called a *supra*. This section provides details of both the tradition of eating and drinking as well as recommended restaurants and bars in the capital.

Whether you try one of the many Georgian restaurants in the city or are invited to a special party, knowledge of the cuisine is helpful. Georgian food reveals significant subtlety and variety. The country is abundant in agricultural land and freshness is the key component in any dish. Intrinsic ingredients are fish and meat; aubergines and green and red peppers, a variety of nuts particularly walnuts and hazelnuts as well as coriander, parsley, mint and types of basil all topped off with remarkable spices of bewildering variety. The traditional Georgian table broadly has three courses. At a banquet or *supra* the table will be groaning with a variety of starters. As the evening progresses hot dishes are added. The evening finishes with cake and seasonal fruits.

Georgia is considered by some to be where viticulture originated and has played an important role throughout the country's history. Most families particularly in rural areas produce their own vintage. There are a large number of differing varieties and there is also a range of sparkling wines. If you are invited to a Georgian table there is a certain tradition to wine drinking, involving a toasting ritual. As the members of the table gather a toastmaster or *tamada* is chosen. This person, normally a man, effectively conducts the toasting and by doing so formulates the dinner table conversation. Among the subjects covered by the *tamada* are toasts to peace, to the reason for meeting, to the host or hostess, to ancestors and parents, to Georgia, to friends, to those who have died, to life, to children, to women, to love, to God and finally to future meetings. Often the *tamada* will toast each individual around the table. Often the *tamada* will say the word *alaverdi*. At this point the person he turns to is expected to develop the theme of the toast and turn it in a new direction. Another feature of toasting is the word *bolomde*. At this point you are expected to drink to the bottom of the glass. If you are fortunate or not depending upon your disposition, a *khantsi* or ram's horn will be taken out, filled with wine and passed around the table. This again you should drain to the last. Women it should be pointed out are not required to keep pace with men.

There are numerous dishes that compromise Georgian cuisine. The following provides descriptions of the array one is likely to encounter. Starters include **Badrijani**

Nigvzit. This is aubergine served cold and filled with a walnut and garlic paste. **Gadazelili** is cheese with mint. **Jigari**, that also means crazy, is a spicy beef salad. No Georgian table is ever complete without some form of **Khachapuri**. The most common variety is a round dough pie filled with cheese. This goes under the name of *Imereuli* as it originated in Imeretia in Western Georgia. Other varieties are: *Adjaruli* – an open boat shaped dough with cheese and topped with an egg, *Achma* – thin layers of boiled dough and cheese with butter, *Penovani* – thin layers of dough with Sulguni cheese, *Megruli* – a larger version of Imereuli with a sprinkling of cheese on top, *Lobiani* – similar to *Imereuli* but with mashed red beans instead of cheese, *Kubdari* or *Svanuri* – rounded dough with a filling of meat, herbs and spices. **Lobio** means beans in Georgian and when on a menu implies red kidney beans served hot in a clay pot with herbs. **Matsoni** is fermented yoghurt. **Mchadi** is a type of corn bread very common in Western Georgia. **Pkhali** comes in two different guises either green or red. The green is cooled spinach, while the red is beetroot leaves. Both are mixed with ground walnuts, spices and garlic and often topped with pomegranate seeds. **Sadili** is a collection of fresh herbs typically, red basil, spring onions, tarragon, parsley and coriander. **Satsivi** is cold turkey or chicken pieces in a walnut sauce with saffron. **Zamtris pamidori** are pickled green

tomatoes stuffed with herbs. **Nadugi** is a soft cream cheese often served with mint. **Sulguni** is a cheese a little harder than Mozzarella and normally slightly salty. **Tushuri** is a hard goat's cheese from the Tusheti region.

Main courses compromise **Adjapsandali** that is a ratatouille with the principal ingredient being aubergine. **Bozbashi** is a lamb stew. **Chakapuli** is also a type of lamb stew but with green plums and fresh tarragon and other herbs. **Chakhokhbili** is a chicken stew with tomatoes and onions and lots of fresh coriander. **Chanakhi** comes in a clay pot and is made of lamb, aubergines, potatoes and tomatoes. **Chashushuli** is a beef stew along with onions and tomato. **Chizhipizhi** is a simple omelette with vegetables. **Chkmeruli** is a dish of chicken pieces cooked on a clay dish with an accompanying garlic sauce. **Ghomi** is essentially cornmeal with a cheese like Sulguni wrapped in it. It is also called Elargi. **Gochi** in Georgian means pig and when served is a roast suckling pig, normally served with the pig's head. **Khinkali** are a meal in themselves. Put simply they are herbed meat either lamb, pork or beef inside a bell shaped dumpling. They should be eaten with a liberal sprinkling of freshly ground pepper. **Kupati** are herbed sausages. **Mtsvadi** is any type of meat cooked on a skewer over an open fire, often with tomatoes and onions. **Mtsvane Lobio Kvertskhit** are green beans with eggs. **Soko** are mushrooms in

Georgian and are normally baked on a *ketsi* (a clay dish). **Shemtsvari Lobio** are sauté green beans with herbs. **Tabaka** is a roasted chicken pressed flat in a clay dish. **Tolma** are stuffed vine leaves. Finally **Tsitsila Shkmerulat** is quail in a rich garlic sauce.

There are a number of sauces and condiments that accompany both starters and main courses. **Adjika** is a fiery normally red condiment originally from Abkhazia made of red chilli, peppers and herbs. It is normally eaten with meat. **Bazha** is a ground walnut paste with walnut oil, water and secret Georgian spices (every cook has their own variety) normally eaten with poultry. **Tkemali** is a plum sauce either red or green with added spices particularly with meat. **Masharapi** is a pomegranate dressing normally eaten with roast sturgeon.

Normally the Georgian meal finishes with fresh fruit, perhaps cake and coffee or tea. Coffee is generally of the Turkish variety. Georgians are not great desert eaters. Occasionally you may find **Churchkhela**. This is grape skins and walnuts, strung on a thread. **Gozinaki** is honey and sugar poured over walnuts.

WINE

Georgia does not yet have an appelation contrôlée. That said most wines are more than pleasant and some are excellent and through companies such as Georgian Wines and Spirits the quality is improving. Naturally farmers sell their own particular vintage and if you have your own container it is quite possible to purchase a good wine very cheaply. If buying in bottles one should expect to pay five lari upwards to ensure that you are purchasing the genuine article. There are cases of forgery and it is probably better to buy only in supermarkets and specialist outlets. Tbilisi itself has its own winery on Melikishvili Street that used to house a museum. There are still some very fine vintages among the 140,000 bottle collection, sometimes for sale.

TABLE WINES

The following provides the different types you are likely to encounter or may wish to order. The most locally famous dry white is **Tsinandali** made from Rkatsiteli and Mtsvane grapes. It matures for three years in oak barrels and when matured is straw coloured with a light fruity taste. Among other dry whites are **Gurjaani** a light golden wine with a slightly bitter taste; **Manavi** a clear soft wine with a good balanced flavour, **Napareuli** a pale straw coloured wine with a light fruity taste and **Rkatsiteli** a dark almost amber coloured wine fermented in clay jars underground that has a smooth aftertaste. All these wines are from the Kakheti region of the country. Other dry whites include **Bacchus**, **Vazisubani** made from the Rkatsiteli and Mtsvane grapes and two wines from the beer brewery Castel called **Shilda** and **Ar Daidardo**. There is a semi-dry white wine called **Sachino**.

It is also possible to buy a range of semi-sweet whites. **Akhmeta** has a light sweetness and is from Kakheti. **Chkhaveri** from Western Georgia is a pale wine with a slight pinkish colour while **Tetra** from Racha is a naturally sweet wine with a light and delicate taste. **Alaznis Veli** from the Alazani Valley in Kakheti is a rich semi sweet.

Turning to the red wines, **Mukuzani** is a very dry red made from the Saperavi grape. **Alexandreuli** from Racha region in Western Georgia is well bodied with a peppery taste and currently considered the pick of the reds. **Tamada Saperavi** is robust and flavoursome with a scent of sour plums. Also from the Saperavi grape is **Old (Dzveli) Tbilisi** that is similar to the Hungarian Bull's Blood. It is heavily tannic and has a spicy bouquet. **Aladasturi** is a peppery red that improves as one makes one's way through the bottle. **Saperavi** from the grape of the same name is an eminently drinkable wine. Other dry reds include **Nekresi**, a Merlot from Lechkhumi and **Teliani** that is a dark amber colour with a slightly astringent taste. If you can find an older bottle the **Kvareli** is considered an excellent vintage dry red. Made from Saperavi grapes it is matured for three years in oak barrels. It has the colour of pomegranates with a heady aroma and bouquet. Not far behind is the red **Napareuli**. Final mention in the dry red category goes to **Chateau Zegaani** described as similar to a full-bodied claret, both subtle and fruity with a ripe berry character.

In the semi sweet category of red wines the main favourites are **Khvanchkara** and **Kindzmareuli**. The former is a natural sweet wine made from a combination of Alexandruli and Mujhuretuli grapes cultivated in Western Georgia. It has a dark ruby colour with a potent aroma. Kindzmareuli is from the Kareli district of Kakheti and produced from the Saperavi grape. It has the look of a rich burgundy and is full bodied. A lighter semi sweet is **Akhasheni** from the Gurjaani district of Kakheti while the **Alaznis Veli** is a good deal stronger but pleasant on the palette. Other semi sweets of note are **Odjaleshi** that has a ruby colour and **Tvishi**.

DESSERT AND FORTIFIED WINES

There are a number of good dessert wines. **Tbilisuri** is considered the king but may be difficult to find. **Kardanakhi** is a white amber coloured wine with a distinct honey fragrance. **Anaga** is similar to a Madeira. Other dessert whites from Kakheti include **Sighnaghi** and **Iveria** while from the west of the country comes **Kolkheti**. In the red department there is the Sameba a port like wine, and **Khilchvi**, **Saamo** and **Salkhino**. There is also a dessert wine named after Tbilisi's most famous artist **Pirosmani**.

SPIRITS

While Georgia does produce vodka and there are a variety of different types quite often named after prominent public figures in Georgia, the main spirit is brandy. These brandies rival those of Armenia and some would argue even French cognac. When looking for a vintage the age of the brandy is important. The following list may prove helpful:

Vardzia - twenty five years.
Sakartvelo - twenty years.
Tbilisi - fifteen to twenty years.
Eniseli - twelve to fifteen years.
Dzalian Dzveli - twelve years.
Abkhazeti - ten years.
Kazbegi - ten years.
Gremi - six to seven years.
Egrisi - six years.
Georgian Brandy - three to five years.

Since independence one name has been revived, that of Sarajishvili. This is a quite excellent brandy.

BEERS

Tbilisi now boasts a highly reputable line in beers produced by the Castel Company. Brands are Argo, Castel, Kazbegi, Porter and Topadze, the latter named after the owner of the company to celebrate his six-tieth birthday. In a matter of two-three years these beers have taken over from Heineken and Turkish beers as the favoured choice.

SOFT DRINKS

As the country is predominantly agricul-tural there has been until recently an untapped potential to produce fruit juices. Fortunately there are a number of compa-nies that now produce fruit juices, just about all of which are 100% natural. Among the fruits now in juice form are, Apple, Orange, Peach, Apricot and Sour Cherry. Mention should be made of Laghidze Waters - a mix of specially pre-pared powders mixed with water, typically lemonade, chocolate or tarragon.

MINERAL WATER

The name Borjomi - a spa town in the central south of the country has been syn-onymous with mineral water in Georgia for many years. **Borjomi** is very high in miner-al content and is thus considered good for medicinal purposes, although perhaps should be drunk in moderation. If during the Soviet period Borjomi held a virtual monopoly not only in Georgia but throughout the former Union, since inde-pendence a number of rivals have entered the market. Among them are **Nabeghlavi** also fizzy, **Caucasian Spring**, both fizzy and still and **Gewa**. As with wine it is bet-ter to purchase mineral waters in super-markets as there are a number of fakes around, that turn out to be no better than tap water.

RESTAURANTS

Over the past few years a veritable plethora of restaurants and bars have sprung up all over the city. Some do not last too long while others change their name as they move under new ownership. It is wise to be a little cautious of small cafés and restaurants. Health and sanitary control is still in its infancy and particularly during the high summer months product freshness cannot be guaranteed. In most restaurants and bars there will be a menu in English, although there is often some amusement in the description of some of the dishes. Most waiters and waitresses speak some English, French or German. Prices naturally vary but are always indicated on the menu. A typical meal with wine will cost in the region of eight to fifteen dollars.

THE OLD TOWN

Argo Bar and Restaurant at 19 Erekle II Street *Tel. 999723* serves Georgian cuisine and is unusual for having goldfish swimming below your feet. The **Borani** restaurant *Tel. 935546* is a floating raft that each evening wends out into the Mtkvari river. The food is traditional Georgian and provides a great opportunity to see the sights of Tbilisi while dining at the same time. You can pick up the Borani from beneath the Metechi Bridge. It is best to phone first to check departure times. Just above the Metechi Church is the **Dzveli Metechi** at 3 Metechi Street *Tel. 744407*. This is a Georgian restaurant and the food is generally excellent. In the summer months, you can dine out on a balcony above the river and take in some splendid views of the Old Town including the Narikala Fortress. The **Golden Fleece** 55 Silver (*Vertskhli*) Street *Tel. 978777* is a reasonably priced family run affair that serves mainly Western Georgian dishes. The restaurant has three

rooms and hence it's possible to be quite private. The decor is a little limited but this is made up for by the food. **Journalists** at 5 Erekle II Square *Tel. 984616* is a relic of the Soviet era. Essentially the restaurant of the Union of Journalists, it still offers a ten percent discount for the profession. **Khachapuri** also called Georgian National Dishes at 1 Leselidze Street is a small café that offers just about every different type of Khachapuri possible. It is open from early morning until early evening. **Mamma Rosa** at 31 Bath (*Abano*) Street *Tel. 753081* is an authentic Italian restaurant. Some consider the prices a little high but the setting is delightful, particularly if you are on the balcony adjacent to the Orbeliani bath house. **Millennium** at 17 Baratashvili Street *Tel. 921117* is a slightly brash city style restaurant serving Georgian and international cuisine. **Mirage** on Bath (*Abano*) Street is a converted bath house that serves Imeretian and West Georgian cuisine. It is the last bath house at the top of the street on the left. It is run by two brothers one of whom was chef to Eduard Shevardnadze's when he was Soviet Foreign Minister. The restaurant conjures up a wonderful atmosphere of the Caucasus being decorated with carpets and other artefacts of the region. In winter months there is an open fire and you can watch your shashlik of pork, beef or a particular favourite roast sturgeon being cooked in front of you. They also produce their own wine that is well worth trying.

Mukhrantubani 23 Baratashvili Street *Tel. 997474* is in an elegant nineteenth century house by the city walls. The front court-yard with a small rose garden is a delight-ful setting in summer. The cuisine is Georgian and with a number of private rooms is a popular haunt for business lunches and dinners. **Narinji** at 9 Baratashvili Street is a day and night time bar, with a summer terrace and for the winter months a cavern built into the city walls. **Nikala Bread House** 7 Gorgasali Street *Tel. 750094* is rumoured to be where khinkhali was invented. Today the restaurant serves traditional Georgian food and there is also a hotel and a bakery that makes bread in the traditional style. **Old Love** 18 Shavteli Street *Tel. 936569* oppo-site Anchiskhati used to be an oriental sweet shop but now is a restaurant that serves a mix of Georgian and international cuisine. **Sachashnico** at 4 Nakashidze Street *Tel. 995857* although the actual entrance is on Baratashvili Street, is a con-verted wine cellar that is deeply evocative of the Caucasus. It is a particularly good place for large gatherings and serves typi-cal Georgian cuisine and in the evenings normally has live music. **Sans Souci** at 13 Shavteli Street *Tel. 986594* is a slightly bohemian style café perfect for a glass of wine looking over Anchiskhati and before or after a visit to the Gabriadze Puppet theatre below. The best spot is the bal-cony, particularly on a summer evening. **Zur Glocke** at 17 Baratashvili Street *Tel.*

921916 is built into the old city walls and serves German and Georgian cuisine with soups a specialty. They also have a good selection of old vintage Georgian wines. While it is just off the old town in the Avlabari district it is worth mentioning the restaurants of the Sheraton Metechi Hotel. On the top floor of the hotel is the **King Gorgasali** Restaurant that apart from offer-ing terrific views of the city, also has a var-ied menu with prices to match. In the hotel foyer is the **Slammers** bar with a Tex-Mex flavour. Also on the ground floor is the **Narikala** Restaurant that offers Georgian and international cuisine. In the summer there is a pool terrace where there is often a barbeque. All the restaurants are open to anyone and can be booked on *Tel. 946444*. Opposite the hotel on Ketevan the Martyr Avenue at 29a is another restaurant called **Mirage** *Tel. 773614*. A summer terrace overlooks the river, the fare is Georgian and international.

CENTRE, MTATSMINDA AND SOLOLAKI

The **Argo** Bar at 24 Rustaveli Avenue serves a near perfect khinkali that more than makes up for the decor. There is a brand new **Chinese Restaurant** at 23 Pushkin Street. It opened in October 2000. **Dukani** 1 Jorjadze Street *Tel. 989839* is opposite Kvashveti church on a side street and offers inexpensive, simple and straightforward Georgian cooking but in a delightful atmosphere. The central log fire makes this an ideal place in the autumn and winter months. The **Green Bar** 16

Rustaveli Avenue *Tel. 997280* by contrast is an up-market city style bar and also serves snacks. The **Kazbegi Bar** 12 Dadiani Street *Tel. 920151* is part of a local chain serving Georgian dishes at very reasonable prices. The owner of Kazbegi is the local brewer king and the restaurants are designed mainly for Georgians to eat out in a setting that is both affordable and of reasonable quality. On both counts the chain is a success. This particular restaurant is rumoured to be the owner's favourite. **Le Creperie** 14 Ingorokva Street *Tel. 922887* as its names suggests has excellent crepes with many different fillings to choose from. This is something of an artistic haunt. **Marco Polo** 44 Rustaveli Avenue *Tel. 935383* is a flashy restaurant that serves international and Georgian dishes in a MTV 'to be seen' environment. The **Mingrelian** Restaurant at 10 Virsaladze Street is a small family run establishment that serves spicy Western Georgian food. **Nikala** at 22 Rustaveli Avenue *Tel. 998283* is Tbilisi's answer to fast food. **Tbiliseli** on Chonkadze Street is something of a secret haunt. It is a little difficult to find, but is up the path from the World Bank headquarters. The restaurant offers spectacular views of the city from the balcony and splendid Georgian cuisine. **Titanic** 16 Rustaveli Avenue *Tel. 935009* is appropriately underground and specialises in fish and seafood. The **Turkish Restaurant** *Tel. 996364* is beneath Republican Square in the underground complex. At the time of writing it is the only Turkish restaurant in town and along with mainstream Turkish food there is also belly dancing most evenings. The **White Crow** at 9 Dadiani Street, behind city hall offers Georgian and European dishes in a friendly atmosphere.

VERA

Belinski Eight at 8 Tamar Chovelidze Street is a bar that also offers quite a diverse range of food, steaks being a particular specialty. **Cantina** at 24 Akhvlediani Street *Tel. 999799* is a small pizzeria that in addition has Georgian food. **Coffee House** at 44 Kostava Street as its name suggests is a daytime place for coffee and cakes. **Csaba's Jazz Rock Café** at 3 Vashlovani Street *Tel. 923192*, just off Akhvlediani street is a good quality Hungarian restaurant and there is often live music. **Dimas** 15 Akhvlediani Street was one of the very first post-communist bars in the city. Along with drinks there is also a limited menu and in the back a garden for the summer months. **El Depo** at 10 Gambashidze Street *Tel. 290661* started life as a Mexican restaurant but is now a khinkali joint. **Gircha** at 31 Melikishvili Street *Tel. 252536* is a summer café for the young university jet-set. The cuisine is basic Georgian. **Gustav** 47 Melikishvili Street *Tel. 292813* is a small café and restaurant close to the university. The **Internet Café** at 18 Akhvlediani Street *Tel. 986954* offers the opportunity to get on-line and have a drink or snack at the same time. The **Kazbegi** restaurant at 8/2

Melikishvili Street *Tel. 995612* is part of the Kazbegi chain. **Le Cabernet** at 8 Tatishvili (*Kazbegi*) Street *Tel. 225865* is a delightful and elegant French restaurant that maintains consistently high standards. **Lino** at 17 Akhvlediani Street is a small bar that also serves international and Georgian cuisine. **McDonald's** on Rustaveli Square needs little introduction here. **Manhattan** at 8 Vashlovani Street is a popular bar particularly for parliamentarians. **Matrioshka** at 5 Makashvili Street serves powerful Russian cocktails. **Metro** at 11 Akhvlediani Street goes through phases of being open and then closes for a couple of months. Essentially a late night bar it also serves food. The **Musa Hotel Restaurant** 27 Kostava Street *Tel. 988815* is the hotel's restaurant but run independently. Offerings are international and Georgian. The **Nali** 4 Kiacheli Street *Tel. 986859* is a small bar and has live music each evening. **Nord West** at 8 Vashlovani Street *Tel. 923271* is another little bar just off Akhvlediani Street. **Nostalgia** at 9 Akhvlediani Street *Tel. 986925* is an up-market restaurant serving Georgian and international cuisine. **Ovatio** 21 Akhvlediani Street *Tel. 931084* is an excellent small restaurant with both international and Georgian dishes. **Pasta and Pizza** 32 Barnov Street *Tel. 982982* is a German owned pizzeria, with authentic pizzas, pastas and German sausage. There is a front courtyard and it proves a popular place for the ex-pat community. **Picasso** 13

Miminoshvili Street *Tel. 989086* on a side street by Babylon Supermarket is Chinese and offers exceptional value for money and the menu is constantly evolving. **Rainer's Café** 39 Barnov Street *Tel. 995429* is a more up-market version of the Pasta and Pizza restaurant owned by the same proprietor. **Sakartvelo** at 12 Melikishvili Street *Tel. 221334* is a large slightly Soviet style restaurant but has an impressive menu. **Samaia** *Tel. 920402* on Elbakidze Rise down the steps from Republican Square has Georgian cuisine. In the winter there is a cosy fireplace while in the summer there is the opportunity for al fresco eating beside a playing fountain. **Sancho** 23 Akhvlediani Street *Tel. 982598* is a small bar that attempts, not very successfully, Spanish cuisine. **Santa Fé** at 20 Akhvlediani Street *Tel. 935848* is a Mexican restaurant. It is very popular with Georgian couples for spicy food with a difference. **Stones** 17 Akhvlediani Street *Tel. 923574* is something of an innovation in Tbilisi. Here you are given a warm stone where you can prepare beef, pork, prawns and the like to your own taste. There are also fondues. **Success** is a new bar just off Akhvlediani Street on Vashlovani Street. It has an interesting decor, particularly the tables. The menu is a mix of Georgian and international. **Taj Mahal** at 17 Akhvlediani Street *Tel. 995632 or (899) 568713* is currently the only genuine Indian restaurant in the city. They also have a Chinese menu and provide a take-away service. **Toucan** 8 Kiacheli

Street *Tel. 908240* is perhaps the pick of the bars around the Vera district. Always popular, the food both Georgian and international is consistently good and the prices are moderate. There is also live Latin American music most evenings. **Wheels** 16 Akhvlediani Street *Tel. 988733* is the definitive ex-pat bar in Tbilisi.

VAKE

Albatros Café 46 Chavchavadze Avenue *Tel. 225258* is a bistro type café serving Italian food and hamburgers. **Amarcord** 90 Paliashvili Street *Tel. 291501* serves Georgian and international cuisine in a cosy atmosphere, with a grand piano and many old photographs lining the walls. The **Art Bar** at 22 Chavchavadze Avenue is a small bar for drinks, snacks and coffee. The **Bangkok Kitchen** 37a Chavchavadze Avenue *Tel. 292734* is a Thai restaurant and as well you can order a Thai massage. **Batonebi** 3 Chavchavadze Avenue 1st Alley *Tel. 250669* is a bakery come café that serves a good pizza and is ideal for lunchtime dining. The **Cocktail Bar** at 20 Chavchavadze Avenue has every imaginable cocktail and also a selection of coffee. **Coffee House** next door at 22 Chavchavadze Avenue is a popular daytime haunt for students and the young Vake set. **El Dorado** 11 Shrosha Street *Tel. 221019* is a restaurant designed in the style of nineteenth century Tbilisi. The food is good and the design even better. **Excess** 2 Chavchavadze Avenue is a popular drinking spot near the university. **Favorite** 42 Chavchavadze Avenue is a small café for coffee and drinks. **German Butcher** 12 Chavchavadze Avenue *Tel. 251510* has meatloaf and sausages and is owned by the same proprietor as the Pizza and Pasta on Barnov Street in Vera. **Gloria** 10 Chavchavadze Avenue is yet another small bar on Vake's main street. **Hunter's Hut** 18 Ateni Street just off Chavchavadze Avenue accessible by the underpass is an Irish style pub that also serves food. **Kazbegi Bar** 50 Chavchavadze Avenue tends to go under the name of its address and is part of the Kazbegi chain of restaurants. **Megobari** 3 Chavchavadze Avenue is a café for the summer and serves Georgian cuisine. **Moulin Rouge** at 11 Mosashvili Street *Tel. 225492* has international and Caucasian cuisine with a 'New Georgian' feel. **Rachisubani** 1 Kus Tba is near the Ethnographic Museum *Tel. 235321* and is another summer restaurant and being slightly out of the city one can escape some of the city heat. There is a balcony for looking over the city below. The cuisine is Georgian. **Sakachapuri** at 33 Paliashvili Street *Tel. 2560* (*only four digits*) has the best khachapuri in the city and serves all the different varieties. **Smuggler's Inn** at 42 Chavchavadze Avenue is a British run bar with a dart board and serves English style pub food.

OTHER DISTRICTS

Other parts of Tbilisi are less well served with restaurants and bars. However it is possible to pick out a few. In Saburtalo **Jamaican Pizza** 9 Vazha Pshavela Avenue

Tel. 379737 is a pizzeria with seafood specialties and has a home delivery service. **Lotos Café** at 25 Gamsakhurdia Avenue *Tel. 380805* is Tbilisi's first and only fully vegetarian restaurant. **Pizzeria Prego** 2a Vazha Pshavela Avenue *Tel. 376710* produces authentic pizza and pasta and has home deliveries. **Stuttgart** 2 Vazha Pshavela Avenue *Tel. 372513* is a German style restaurant in the heart of Saburtalo. By the river bank **Atlantida** 6 Right Bank *Tel. 982378* serves European and Georgian cuisine with an emphasis on fish and seafood. Similarly **Maiko's Fish Tavern** 8 Orbeliani Street *Tel. 936399* as its name suggests is a fish restaurant, some directly from the Mtkvari. The restaurant also has live music and a garden dining area. Across the river in Didube **Café Alba** 3 Marjanishvili Street is a small café serving Georgian cuisine. **Café Luxe** 86-90 Aghmashenebeli Avenue, actually in Marjanishvili Square is a self-service diner. In Marjanishvili Square there is another **McDonald's.**

ACCOMMODATION

Tbilisi now boasts a surprisingly large number of small hotels and guest houses. Refugees occupy most of the main Soviet era larger hotels. Typically hotels charge between $50-$150 per night. However it is worth shopping around and bargaining to some extent. Depending upon one's length of stay it is quite possible to receive a discount of as much as fifty percent. The city's hotel keepers are eager for business and will do as much as they can to accommodate your requirements. It is also quite possible to stay with families although there is no formal system for arranging this. Due to the unpredictable nature of the city's electricity system, all hotels should have their own generator. Longer term visitors may well wish to rent an apartment or house.

OLD TOWN AND AVLABARI
Bread House Hotel 7 Gorgasali Street
Tel. 999537 Fax 985424
A converted bakery with a popular restaurant. Prices from $70-$100 per night.

Dzveli Metechi Hotel 3 Metechi Rise
Tel. 990536 Fax 997843
Fifteen roomed hotel with stunning views of the sulphur baths and Narikala. Prices from $60.

Dzveli Ubani Hotel 5 Dumas Street
Tel. 922404 Fax 922464
In the heart of the Old Town six rooms with prices from $70-$110 per night.

Georgian House 38 Vakhtang VI Street
Tel. 791919 Fax 791920
Nine roomed hotel in the heart of Avlabari.

Mtis Broli 4 Elene Akhvlediani Rise
Tel. 940604 Fax 940604
Former state run now private guesthouse close to the river. Singles $40, Doubles $50.

Sharmi Hotel 11 Chakhrukhadze Street
Tel. 986348 Fax 985333
Six roomed hotel in the old town with prices from $60 - $100 per night.

Sheraton Metechi Palace 20 Telavi Street
Tel. 946444 Fax 956135
The main hotel of the city with some 247 rooms and a five star rating. The hotel has a number of restaurants, a business centre, swimming pool and all the other facilities one would expect from a quality hotel chain.

VIP Hotel 31 Leselidze Street
Tel. 989809 Fax 920040
Eight single and double rooms in the heart of the old town, ranging in price from $60-$120 with an extra $10 for meals.

CENTRE, MTATSMINDA AND SOLOLAKI

Bomond 11 Alexander Chavchavadze St
Tel. 986003 Fax 996246
Eight roomed hotel just off Rustaveli Avenue that charges $90-$120 per night.

Diplomat 4 Bolo Aghmarti (nr. Amaghleba St.)
Tel. 922088 Fax 923746
Email hoteldip@hotmail.com
Pleasant hotel close to Freedom Square with all modern conveniences.

Ipari 4 Abashidze Street (by Opera House)
Tel. 996799 Fax 990751
Small family run hotel with six rooms with prices from $100-$150.

Keria Guest House 52 Rustaveli Avenue
Tel. 931444
Eight rooms right in the centre by the Rustaveli monument with prices at $80-$90.

Lia 35 Arsena Odzelashvili Street
Tel. 984443 Fax 984443
Five rooms recently renovated with a communal balcony. $90-$120 per night.

Marriott Hotel Tbilisi
Hotel Tbilisi was destroyed during the civil war in 1992. It is due to reopen in spring 2001 as a five star hotel. A further hotel is being built on Freedom Square due to open in late 2001.

Merani 42 Rustaveli Avenue
Tel. 932378 Fax 934675
Centrally located, seven en suite rooms and satellite television. Prices start at $90 per night with special deals for longer stays.

Mimi 36 Brothers Zubalishvili Street
Tel. 921880 Fax 941430
English speaking with airy rooms, two with en suite facilities. Six double rooms. Also free use of computer. Prices $50-$120.

Mtatsminda Hotel 6 Chitadze Street
Tel. 989455
Fourteen rooms owned by the Ministry of Foreign Affairs $50-$70 per night.

Mtis Kalta 46 Arsena Odzelashvili Street
Tel. 936397 Fax 923435
Four rooms with shared facilities, billiard room and pleasant shared living room. $90 per night including breakfast and lunch.

Sanapiro Hotel 12 Brosse Street
Tel. 934746 Fax 934746
Well run hotel close to the river with prices from $100-$120 per night.

Tori Hotel 10 Chanturia Street
Tel. 923765 Fax 923822
Turkish purpose built hotel that opened in 2000. The hotel has a sauna, billiard room and you can also order a Turkish bath. Prices start from $90 per night.

VERA AND VAKE
Argo 1 Kobuleti Lane
Tel. 230673, 227624 Fax 253303
Email argo@access.sanet.ge
Twelve rooms with English speaking owners and a pleasant dining room with prices from $90-$110.

Atlanta 13 Rcheulishvili Street
Tel. 235985 Fax 292912
Twelve rooms in upper Vera overlooking the city from $70-$120 per night.

Betsy's 21 Gogebashvili Street
Tel. 989553, 983551 Fax 001237
Email betsy@2121.ge
Fifteen rooms beautifully decorated with a feel for the Caucasus but with western comfort in mind. There is also a roof-top bar and restaurant available to all. Much loved by the American diplomatic and business communities and as such places are at a premium. Prices start at $90 plus VAT.

Classic Hotel 18 Inola Gurgelia Street
Tel. 227415 Fax 227415
Email bclassic44@hotmail.com
Five rooms in a quiet street in Vera with prices at $60-$95 including breakfast and dinner.

Demi Hotel 10 Ananuri Street
Tel. 220619 Fax 252321
Seven roomed hotel in a quiet corner of Vera from $100-$120 per night.

Diplomat Hotel 34 Shanidze Street
Tel. 252712 Fax 292757
Email diplomat@gw.acnet.ge
Five roomed hotel with prices from $60-$100 including breakfast and dinner.

Iliani Guest House 1 Veriko Anjaparidze St.
Tel. 234086 Fax 225676
Pleasantly designed seven roomed house currently undergoing expansion, single and double rooms from $70-$100.

Kartli 37 Barnov Street
Tel. 982966 Fax 999134
Email saktours@kartli.com.ge
German run hotel with pleasant rooms from $60.

Kolkhi Guest House 31 Shanidze Street
Tel. 234093 Fax 234093
Ever expanding guesthouse with en suite facilities, balconies and shared sitting room with open fire and office facilities. English spoken. Prices from $40-$90.

Liza Guest House 23 Kereselidze Street
Tel. 920595 Fax 931655
Email liza2323@access.sanet.ge
Very pleasant hotel with prices from $100.

Metro Hotel 16 Kobuleti Street
Tel. 294647 Fax 290341
Seven rooms and satellite television and computer usage. Prices range from $80-150.

Musa Hotel 27 Kostava Street
Tel. 988815 Fax 933265
Eleven rooms by the Philharmonic hall, the better rooms are away from the main street, prices $50-$75, breakfast an additional $5.

Nia 16 Zemo Vake Street
Tel. 291103 Fax 234068
Three single rooms and two suites overlooking the city with prices from $60-$100.

Vake Guest House 80 Chavchavadze Ave.
Tel. 292873
Old Soviet style guest house at $15 per night.

Vera Inn Hotel 53 Barnov Street
Tel. 291252 Fax 291252
Three rooms with prices from $50 per night.

Vera Palace Hotel 24/8 Kuchishvili Street
Tel. 253340 Fax 221298
Modern purpose built hotel with twenty-one rooms Singles at $132, doubles $168.

Victoria Hotel 42 Petriashvili Street
Tel. 291269 Fax 294450
Email victoria@global-erti.net
Nine roomed converted house, elegantly designed. Prices from $80-$120 and breakfast lunch and dinner an additional $10.

SABURTALO
Adjara Hotel 1 Constitution Square
Tel. 334360 Fax 333105
Soviet built hotel in which floors five and seven are available, the remaining floors are full of refugees. A cheap alternative at $50 per night but not recommended for long stays.

Batesta Guest House 52 Saburtalo Street
Tel. 390116 Fax 536015
Email batesta@access.sanet.ge
10 roomed hotel in a quiet part of town. Prices start at $50 plus $10 for meals.

California Guest House 157 Nutsubidze St.
Tel. 320514 Fax 320514
Seven roomed hotel from $60-$100 per night.

Iberia Inn 8-10 Bakhtrioni Street
Tel. 967548 Fax 940718
Eight very large rooms all well apportioned. The hotel also has conference facilities, restaurant, and bar. Prices start at $200.

Khedi Hotel 63/2 Zemo Vedzisi Street
Tel. 380416 Fax 995588
Sixteen rooms in the heart of Saburtalo with prices ranging from $60-$85 per night. The hotel also has conference facilities.

Lago Guest House 27 Kandelaki Street
Tel. 374210 Fax 967133
Well designed and maintained in a quiet suburb.

Lali Hotel 60 Mitskevich Street
Tel. 371174 Fax 379933
Bright hotel in Saburtalo with sauna and swimming pool. Six rooms from $90-$110 per night.

Medea Hotel 40 Mitskevich Street
Tel. 370125 Fax. 941243
Pleasant hotel with six rooms, two doubles. Prices are $70-$90 per night.

Sairme Hotel 110 Burdzgla Street
Tel. 220974 Fax 225117
Twelve roomed hotel with prices between $70-$130.

Sympatia Hotel 4 Gagarin Street First Alley
Tel. 370590 Fax 995588
Twenty six rooms in a very pleasant location, with two swimming pools, sauna, training room, a restaurant and conference facilities.

Tamuna Guest House 23 Kandelaki Street
Tel. 233432 Fax 969777
Well run hotel with fourteen rooms and a sauna. Prices from $80-$130.

Tsitsinatela Hotel 51 Vazha Pshavela Ave.
Tel. 393435 Fax 302656
Sixteen rooms on one of Saburtalo's main thoroughfares at $60-$100 per night.

Villa Berika 9 Dzotsenidze Street
Tel. 942506, Fax 933562
Email berica@Tbilisi-info.net
Delightful hotel above the city, en-suite facilities in all fifteen rooms, sauna, training room, billiards and bar. Prices from $120 upwards.

White Inn Hotel 74 Tsagareli Street
Tel. 381451, Fax 943147
Pleasant hotel in a quiet street from $100 per night.

AGHMASHENEBELI AND DIDUBE
London Hotel 8 Chikobava Street
Tel. 955364 Fax 954381
Five rooms lovingly designed hotel with prices from $120-$170.

Omari Hotel 16 Tsinamdzghvrishvili Street
Tel. 952952, 943001
Small hotel not far from the centre with prices from $50-$70 per night.

COMMUNICATIONS

INTERNET
   For those who do not have a computer there is an Internet Cafe at 18 Akhvlediani Street *(Tel. 986954).* In extremis one can use the facilities of the service providers for a small fee. For those who wish to set up an account there are four main providers in the city.

Sanet 37 Rustaveli Avenue
Tel. 987414, Email info@sanet.ge

Caucasus Net 42 Rustaveli Avenue
Tel. 936013, Email webmaster@caucasus.net

Iberiapac 31 Rustaveli Avenue
Tel. 920087, Email webmaster@iberiapac.ge

Kheta 2a Kazbegi Avenue
Tel. 331274, Email webmaster@kheta.ge

MOBILE
Four companies provide mobile facilities, both for in Georgia calls and international. The companies are:

Geocell 35 Kostava Street
Tel. 922222

GT Mobile 32 Rustaveli Avenue
Tel. 250606

Magticom 21 Chavchavadze Avenue
Tel. 250000 and 253385

Megacom 22 Kostava Street
Tel. 999999

TELEPHONE
   The country code for Georgia is 995 and the city code for Tbilisi is 32. For international calls simply dial 8-10- country code etc. Most telephones are now hooked up for making international calls but if you are staying long term and have rented an apartment it is as well to make sure your landlord has connected the telephone up properly. If you wish to call from the street there are now a number of services along Rustaveli Avenue. The coin operated street telephones are only for calls in the city. Again for those renting apartments, there are two types of telephone charge. The first is the charge for the calls you make. In most of the city, particularly in the centre

calls are free. International, intercity and calls to mobile phones are charged. Payment each month is transacted at the main telecommunications building at 31 Rustaveli Avenue. The second payment is a monthly rental charge for the line. This can be paid in either monthly, or annual instalments. The charge is 2 lari per month. This is payable at 21 Chavchavadze Avenue (not immediately on the street but down a small alley on the right and on the first floor). You are responsible for remembering when to pay, not the telephone company. Occasionally the company may ring with a recorded message in Georgian. If you do not pay the telephone is cut off and it then takes one or two days to reconnect.

POST

The postal system is not reliable. Most people develop their own network for sending letters inside the city and abroad. If you do need to send a letter or parcel the main post office is at forty four David Aghmashenebeli Avenue. If you are receiving mail it is better to use your work address rather than home address. This is purely for the reason that offices in Tbilisi become better known to the postman and in many apartment blocks and houses there are no letterboxes or if there are, they are in such a shabby state that anyone can help themselves to whatever arrives. There are a number of courier or express mail services particularly useful for sending documents and parcels abroad.

DHL 105 Tsereteli Avenue
Tel. 999568

Federal Express 7 Ketevan the Martyr Ave.
Tel. 999042

Georgian EMS 31 Rustaveli Avenue.
Tel. 942020

TNT 3 Anjaparidze Street
Tel. 250328

UPS 47 Kostava Street
Tel. 920356, 920344

ENTERTAINMENT

GUIDES

There is one What's On type guide – *Tbilisi Pastimes* - available from Prospero's Bookshop and a number of bars and hotels.

SEASONS AND TICKETS

The main concert and theatre seasons are the spring March to June and the autumn September to November. Tickets for all events should be purchased from the venue where it is taking place. Opening hours tend to be 11.00am to around 5.00pm. Popular performances can sell out quickly so it is advisable to purchase your tickets one or two days in advance. There is no real concept of booking, nor can credit cards be used.

CINEMA

The city's main cinema is called Twenty First Century (Rustaveli) at 5 Rustaveli Avenue *Tel. 997605*. Renovated in 1999 it shows some of the latest international releases normally dubbed in Russian. Occasionally there are seasons of Georgian films sometimes with English sub-titles. Cinema House normally referred to as Dom Kino at 2 The Brothers Kakabadze Street *Tel. 935615 (dzmebi kakabadzeebis kucha)* near the Academy of Sciences shows more eclectic films and screens more Georgian films. Other cinemas tend to show erotica and mafia films.

CLASSICAL MUSIC AND OPERA

The main concert halls are the Tbilisi Music Centre at 125 Aghmashenebeli Avenue *Tel. 950119*, the Sarajishvili Conservatoire 8 Griboedov Street *Tel. 934624* or *922446* and the Paliashvili Opera House, 25 Rustaveli Avenue Tel. 983248. To find out what is on, it is recommended to go to the relevant venue. At times Georgian works are performed. Particular favourites are *Daisi*, *Absalom & Eteri* and *Kote & Keto* by Paliashvili at the Opera House.

DANCE

Not often in Tbilisi the Georgian State Dance Company should not be missed. Performances are at 17 Rustaveli Avenue. The Opera House quite often hosts classical ballet performances often with virtuosi from the Bolshoi in Moscow or the Mariinsky in Saint Petersburg.

ROCK, JAZZ AND WORLD MUSIC

The Philharmonic Concert Hall, 1 Melikishvili Street is perhaps the main concert hall for more contemporary music. Many of the bars on Akhvlediani Street host live bands (jazz, rock, latin) most evenings. There is a speciality jazz club at the Adjara Hotel in the Saburtalo district of the city, while the Beatles Club on Kostava Street has Georgia's version of the fab four most evenings. At 13 Chardin Street in the Old Town is an Elvis Club. Between the Marjanishvili and Queen Tamar Bridges on the right bank of the river at 8 Sanapiro is the Lemon Club, Tbilisi's closest equivalent to warehouse cult. Occasionally they have latin nights. Best to call 999199 for details. Also on the right bank underneath Heroes Square at 6 Right Bank is the Joy nightclub where many of Tbilisi's elite can be seen. Call 921302 for times and details. *Tbilisi Pastimes* is particularly strong on tracking down local bands. Furthermore the magazine is the organiser of an annual music festival normally held in July.

THEATRE

Tbilisi boasts an extraordinary number of theatres. Performances range from the avant-garde and experimental to the more traditional rendering of Shakespeare, a particular favourite in Georgia and classical Georgian and Russian works. The most famous theatre is the Rustaveli. In both the spring and autumn there tend to be theatre festivals. While most performances are in Georgian it well worth a visit as the performances can be both unusual and at times spectacular. Robert Sturua's *Richard III* at the Rustaveli and the late Tumanishvili's *Midsummer Nights Dream* at the Film Actors Studio are absolute musts, if they are on. The Griboedov Theatre presents Russian classics in Russian and the Armenian Theatre in Avlabari in Armenian, although here you can get a cassette in Russian of performances. There is a strong tradition of puppet theatre and performances are well worth attending. The main theatres are:

Rustaveli Theatre 17 Rustaveli Avenue
Tel. 936583

Marjanishvili Theatre 8 Marjanishvili Street
Tel. 955966

Film Actors Studio 164 Aghmashenebeli Ave.
Tel. 340937

Pantomime Theatre 37 Rustaveli Avenue
Tel. 982506

Dumbadze Theatre 99/1 Aghmashenebeli Ave.
Tel. 950309

Griboedov Theatre 2 Rustaveli Avenue
Tel. 931106

Gabriadze Marionette Theatre 13 Shavteli St.
Tel. 986590

Single Actors Studio 16 Anjaparidze Street
Tel. 221338

Akhmeteli Theatre 8 Vekua Street (Gldani)
Tel. 625973

Basement Theatre 42 Rustaveli Avenue
Tel. 999500

Old House Theatre 1 Metechi Rise
Tel. 770464

Small Theatre 21 Erekle II Street
Tel. 920545

Royal District Theatre 10 Abesadze Street
Tel. 985383

Khorava Actors House 11a Leonidze Street
Tel. 987536

Petre Adamian Armenian Theatre
8 Ketevan the Martyr Ave.
Tel. 744148.

HEALTH AND SAFETY

HEALTH

Medical care in many fields is not yet up to the standard of western countries and so one or two precautions should be taken. Basic advice is to take out full medical insurance before arrival that includes evacuation. It is recommended to have the following jabs or ensure they are up to date: rabies, tetanus, polio, hepatitis, diphtheria and typhoid. This is particularly for travel outside Tbilisi. If one requires medical attention Frontline Medical Services at 2 Arakishvili Street in Vake *Tel. 251941* or *251951* should be the first port of call. This is a private western clinic that offers both emergency care and normal medical services. For those staying for longer periods there is a membership system. They have two emergency numbers *(899) 550911* or *551911* and also have ambulance facilities. For further peace of mind all the staff speak English and there is one expatriate doctor. If one wants to entrust oneself to Georgian medicine then you can call 009 in an emergency or 004 for an ambulance. In both cases you will need someone who speaks either Georgian or Russian. Tbilisi rivals any other city in dentistry and is cheaper than in the West. Some people travel especially to Tbilisi for dental treatment. Two clinics are recommended: Denta+ at 38 Vazha Pshavela Avenue *Tel. 395406* and Dentex at 8 Revaz Laghidze Street (*5th floor*), *Tel. 983990*.

SAFETY

Tbilisi is generally a safe city but normal safety measures should be adopted. If you rent an apartment you may be at some risk as it will become quickly known that a foreigner lives there. It is a good idea to ensure that the apartment has proper security arrangements, bars on windows and a solid door. In the street it is advisable only to take the money you actually require. The city, at least in the centre, is safe at night although again take normal personal security measures.

STAYING HEALTHY

A few safeguards should ensure good health throughout your visit. All fresh produce should be thoroughly washed before consumption. Don't buy snacks from street sellers particularly around the markets. There is no quality control and there have been cases where rat meat has been used in sausages. It is better to boil water before drinking and better to purchase mineral water. There are a number of varieties both still and sparkling.

These are Borjomi, Gewa, and Caucasian Spring. If you travel outside Tbilisi it is a good idea to take a supply with you.

MONEY AND PAYMENTS

BANKS

Banking hours are from 10.00am – 5.00pm and some open on Saturdays. Almost all banks can give you cash from your credit card and the Bank of Georgia on Freedom Square and TBC Bank on Chavchavadze Avenue have ATM machines for credit cards and cirrus. There are also a large number of exchange offices dotted around the city. Rates are displayed on boards. While banks will exchange any currency into lari, the exchange centres will only change dollars and sometimes deutsche marks. If you bring cash into Georgia, dollars are the best and where possible denominations after 1990.

ABSOLUTE BANK 8 Ingorokva St. *Tel. 938922*. Credit cards and travellers' cheques. There is also a branch in the Sheraton Metechi Hotel.
BANK OF GEORGIA 3 Pushkin Street *Tel. 921663*. Credit cards, travellers' cheques, Also has an ATM machine for Visa, MasterCard, Cirrus and Maestro both for dollars and lari.
INTELLECTBANK 127 Aghmashenebeli Ave. *Tel. 942290*. Credit cards and travellers' cheques.
TBC BANK 11 Chavchavadze Avenue *Tel. 220661*. Credit cards, travellers' cheques and an ATM machine for Visa, Mastercard, Cirrus and Maestro that will give you lari only.

TBILCOMBANK 2 Dadiani Street *Tel. 988592.* Credit cards and travellers' cheques.

TBILCREDITBANK 27 Rustaveli Avenue *Tel. 986010.* Credit cards and travellers' cheques.

CREDIT CARDS

Most hotels accept credit cards as do more western orientated shops. Tbilisi is joining the world of plastic so the number of outlets for primarily MasterCard and Visa is expanding. The American Express representative is at 67 Aghmashenebeli Avenue *Tel. 940364.*

CURRENCY

The currency of Georgia is the lari. There are 100, 50, 20, 10, 5, 2 and 1 lari notes. The lari is made up of 100 tetris.

SHOPPING

ART AND ANTIQUES

Tbilisi boasts an extraordinary number of artists. Many of the souvenir shops sell paintings as well. Two particular places for art are the steps of the Academy of Sciences and the park near what is called the Dry Bridge (near the American Embassy). For antiques, a special note must be given to the market adjacent to the park under Dry Bridge close to the American Embassy. Here one can find some extraordinary bargains. It is well worth a visit and is particularly good at weekends. Specialist antique shops can be found between 19 & 21 and 44-46 Rustaveli Avenue and at 10 Aghmashenebeli Avenue. On Marjanishvili Street at number eighteen

is a Tiffany's style jewellery and antique store called Diadema. There are specialist carpet outlets at 38 Rustaveli Avenue, at the top of Gorgasali Square and on the corner of Bath (Abano) Street. For all antiques, including carpets and metalwork you will require a special licence to take it with you when you leave the country. Normally the store holder will assist you with this, but in the case of difficulties consult the Ministry of Culture 37 Rustaveli Avenue.

BOOKS AND NEWSPAPERS

Opened in late 1999 Prospero's in a small courtyard at 34 Rustaveli Avenue is the premier English language bookshop in the city. They stock a wide range of books including a special section on the Caucasus. It is difficult to find English newspapers although the kiosk outside the Rustaveli metro station sells the *Economist.* For local information and news there are two newspapers. *The Georgian Times* is a daily paper but does not reveal very much. Launched in 2000 *Georgia Today* is weekly and better written. *Tbilisi Pastimes* is a weekly listings magazine. Of the many books you will see in Georgian bookshops, the majority in English, French and German are from the Soviet period. The art books are good but the others while revealing some interesting nuggets are mostly 'proletarian' in content. The suggested reading in this book provides details of the major English language literature on Tbilisi and Georgia.

CRAFTS, DESIGN AND GIFTS

Chased metalwork, woodcarving and embroidery are three of the main crafts of Georgia. Rustaveli Avenue hosts a number of specialist souvenir shops. Particularly good is the shop in the underpass near the Opera House. More unusual works can be found at the shop of the Arts and Cultural Centre at 3 Rustaveli Avenue. Another place for souvenirs is the steps of the Academy of Sciences, 56 Rustaveli Avenue and next to the Rustaveli Theatre at 19 Rustaveli Avenue. There is an Art Salon at 12 Baratashvili Street. La Maison Bleue at 26 Belinsky Street,is particularly good for tie-dyed and hand painted scarves

DEPARTMENT STORES

The concrete building at the Freedom Square end of Rustaveli Avenue either side of the Griboedov Theatre is the home of the city's main department store. Over the past ten years it has gone through a fair amount of change. At the time of writing it is the best place for purchasing jewellery (ground floor). On other floors you will find the normal fare for a department store, although the layout may not quite be what one expects.

FASHION

The main shopping avenues, Chavchavadze and David Aghmashenebeli host a burgeoning number of boutiques. At times there are some good bargains on Italian and French designer wear, but normally the prices are excessive. Most

Tbilisians purchase their clothes at what is called the *Bazroba* – an extensive street style market near the main fruit and vegetable market by the main railway station. Here one can find just about anything under the sun. A note of caution - many of the goods, particularly clothes, sold here are not originals. Furthermore the market is extremely crowded at all times and pick pocketing is particularly virulent. That said, for a real flavour of a part of Tbilisi life the *Bazroba* is worth a visit.

FOOD AND DRINK

Each suburb of the city has an open market selling seasonal fruit and vegetables. The main market of the city is close to the football stadium and main railway station in Didube at 137 Tsinamdzghvrishvili Street. An easier to use market is at the bottom of what is still normally referred to as Collective Farm Square (*kolmeurneobis moedani*), but actually Orbeliani Square, at the junction of Vekua and Atoneli Streets. It is on two floors. The ground floor entrance is devoted to fish and vegetables. Upstairs meat, fruit, a variety of cheeses and the Caucasus' famous spices can be purchased. It is always advisable to agree a price before purchasing. There is a knack to bartering. Firstly enquire of the price. If you think it is a bit steep walk a few paces away and you should find the price comes down considerably. Additionally the more you buy the less you pay per kilogramme. It is sometimes difficult to persuade the vendors to sell you half or quarter kilo quantities, although persistence invariably pays dividends. As much of the produce is seasonal prices can vary sharply – even from week to week.

The markets to some extent still convey a sense of the silk route markets of the days of yore and shopping is something of an experience and sometimes baffling. It is as well to be armed with one or two words of one or two languages. The purchase of lettuce and fresh herbs is likely to be conducted in Azeri, Georgian or Russian. This is because the ladies are mainly Azeris from the southeast of the country. Rather than using the lari to count they use either roubles or manats (the currency of Azerbaijan as well as the pre-Soviet currency for the whole Caucasus). When however they use the manat or rouble they mean the lari. Similarly kopeks are tetris. Other sellers will use either Georgian or Russian – probably the latter as they will consider you as a foreigner and hence you are assumed to know Russian.

There are a number of supermarkets. Big Ben at 52 and Eurocentre at 54 Chavchavadze Avenue in the Vake district are among the best as is Babylon at 23 Kostava Street and Euro Gardens at 2 Gudiashvili Street adjacent to the Museum of Georgian Art. Zemeli near the Ministry of Culture, 37 Rustaveli Avenue opened in 2000. Baden-Baden at 90 Aghmashenebeli Avenue has a special selection of locally produced German sausage and cured meat. In smaller shops it is worth checking sell by dates as produce can remain on shelves for long periods.

MUSIC AND VIDEOS

Souvenir shops on Rustaveli Avenue sell Georgian music. Of particular note are the compact discs and tapes of Georgian folk music. The ensembles *Tbilisi* and *Rustavi* are considered among the best. For sacred music the Georgian Orthodox Church shop on Sioni Street is the best bet. Popular Georgian music can be found at all music outlets – either from street vendors or shops. All western music and videos are pirate copies of the originals. Prospero's bookshop provides a rental service of genuine western movies.

TRANSPORT

BUSES AND TROLLEY BUSES

Cheaper than microbuses typically 10-30 tetris buses and trolley buses are a convenient way of moving around the city. They do however tend to be slower and they only stop at specified bus stops. Payment is made directly to the driver. A particularly useful route is the bus to the airport. The number 37 costs fifty tetris and runs from the Railway Station - Queen Tamar Avenue - Kostava Street - Rustaveli Avenue - Freedom Square - Baratashvili Street and then on to the airport. Journey time from the centre is roughly half an hour to forty minutes and they run about every half hour but only during the day and early evening.

CAR HIRE

Both Avis and Hertz have representations in Tbilisi. Avis is at 1 Rustaveli Avenue *Tel. 923594 Fax 923591*, while Hertz is at 5-7 Shavteli Street *Tel. 995003 Fax 995122*. However many people tend to rent both a driver and a car. The travel agencies listed in the useful addresses can arrange this.

FLIGHTS

The city is well served by international flights. Austrian Airways, British Airways, Swiss Air and Turkish Airlines all operate services to Tbilisi. A local company Air Zena operates flights to Amsterdam, Athens, Frankfurt, Kiev, Moscow, Sochi, Tashkent, Tehran, and Tel Aviv. Local newspapers provide the schedules as do a range of web sites. There is a twice-weekly flight to Baku and periodically Air Armenia runs flights to Erevan. If you work for an international organisation it is possible to use the services of the World Food Programme flights to Baku, Erevan and towns in Western Georgia. If you need to contact the airport the general number is 947512. The operators speak Russian and Georgian.

MICROBUSES

Microbuses, also called Mashrutkas are a very convenient way of travelling around the city. The only hurdle to using them is knowledge of the language. However this is easy solved by a guide to the numbering system. Microbuses follow specific routes but can be hailed down anywhere along them. It is only on Rustaveli Avenue that there are specific stopping zones. These are: on the Rustaveli Theatre side – Freedom Square, The Janashia Museum, Rustaveli Theatre, The Opera House and outside the Iveria Hotel. On the other side of the street they will stop at The Ministry of Justice, School Number One, Parliament, and Freedom Square Metro Station. Elsewhere in the city they will stop wherever you want, apart from on bridges.

Typically there is a flat charge of either forty or fifty tetris. The fare is normally indicated on the front window and you pay when you alight. The only word you need to know in Georgian to use them is *gaajaret* meaning stop. To stop a microbus on the street simply hold out your hand. There are no timetables. Essentially they run from sunrise to sunset and until ten to eleven in the evenings and somewhat later during the summer months.

Given the plethora of microbuses the following is a list based upon where you may want to get to from Rustaveli Avenue. As Tbilisi is a city that runs primarily on a East-West axis most routes take in the Centre. Hence if you are on Rustaveli Avenue and want to get to Vake, Vera, Saburtalo and the Left Bank and other western parts be on the Opera House side of the street. For the Old Town, Avlabari, Ortachala and Isani it is best to catch a microbus on the Parliament side. Other routes to specific destinations are additionally listed.

RUSTAVELI AVENUE. –

OLD TOWN
133, 140, 152, 154, 300a.

AVLABARI & ISANI
2a, 4a, 13, 17, 17a, 27, 31, 34, 68, 92, 140, 141, 200a, 227, 231, 234a, 251, 251a, 260, 268.

AGHMASHENEBELI VIA ZAARBRUCHEN SQ.
146.

AGHMASHENEBELI VIA MARJANISHVILI SQ.
31, 40, 68, 94, 110, 145, 231, 209a, 268.

CENTRAL RAILWAY STATION & MARKET
12, 41, 68, 94, 141, 146, 209.

MELIKISHVILI ST. & VAKE
4, 4a, 48, 48a, 74, 136, 145, 170, 201.

SABURTALO (GAMSAKHURDIA AVENUE & VAZHA-PSHAVELA AVENUE)
2, 2a, 13, 17, 17a, 75, 140, 152, 160, 200, 200a, 251, 251a, 260, 275.

SABURTALO (KOSTAVA STREET & SAAKADZE SQUARE)
8, 10, 27, 34, 56, 61, 72, 154, 160, 227, 234a, 248a, 276, 261, 266, 272.

SABURTALO (BAKHTRION STREET)
25, 225.

DIDUBE (TSERETELI AVENUE)
31, 34, 40, 41, 85, 92, 133, 141, 146, 209, 209a, 231, 234a, 285, 300a.

DIGHOMI (CENTRAL BUS STATION)
40, 61, 209a, 261.

GORGASALI STREET & KRTSANISI
8, 140, 248a.

SOLOLAKI
12.

UPPER VERA & VAKE
99, 299.

PUSHKIN SQUARE – AGHMASHENEBELI AVENUE
6, 202.

FREEDOM SQUARE – SABURTALO VIA TABUKASHVILI ST.
22, 254.

LEFT BANK & AGHMASHENEBELI AVENUE - SABURTALO
50, 66, 134, 222, 250.

LEFT BANK & AGHMASHENEBELI AVENUE - VAKE
19, 210a.

RAILWAY STATION - VAKE
9, 59, 208, 259.

RAILWAY STATION - SABURTALO
38, 42, 58, 80, 104, 114, 267, 280, 315.

RAILWAY STATION - AVLABARI VIA AGHMASHENEBELI AVE.
62, 262.

DYNAMO STADIUM - VAKE
9, 32, 104, 126, 208, 232.

DYNAMO STADIUM - SABURTALO
51, 102, 114, 230, 315.

DIDUBE (TSERETELI AVENUE) - VAKE
32, 126, 232.

SABURTALO - VAKE
14, 15, 44, 128, 214, 215, 234.

AVLABARI - OLD TOWN (BREAD SQUARE)
46, 246.

AVLABARI - AGHMASHENEBELI AVENUE
70a, 116, 127.

SPECIFIC ROUTES

RAILWAY STATION - MOUNT LOTKHIN – TBILISI SEA – TEMKA UNIVERSITY SITE 130.

FREEDOM SQUARE - FUNICULAR - GOGEBASHVILI ST
67, 270.

FREEDOM SQUARE - FUNICULAR - VAKE VIA BARNOV STREET 137.

FREEDOM SQUARE - FUNICULAR - DIDUBE BUS STATION 158.

FREEDOM SQUARE - AIRPORT 149.

TAXIS

The city has three forms of taxi. The most prominent are the red Mitsubishi taxis that are metered, when they work. Typically the charge is fifty tetris plus 30 tetris per kilometre. They can be booked on 008 or 921921. Yellow cabs can be booked on 234024 and are equally reliable. There are then a plethora of private cars that double up as taxis. As a rule of thumb any journey in the city centre will cost between two-three laris. Some people prefer to agree a price in advance but the best method is simply to hand a two lari note at the end of the journey and get out. Tipping is not required, the norm is to round up to the nearest whole. Taxi drivers do not have to know 'the knowledge'. As a consequence many may have less idea of where you want to go than you do. This is mainly because street names have changed considerably over the last decade and many drivers are more familiar with the old names. If you know of a particular landmark near where you want to go ask for that and they should know where it is. Taxis to and from the airport are typically between ten to fifteen dollars.

UNDERGROUND

Tbilisi has a fairly good underground system that provides the best means of travelling longer distances in the city. There are two lines that intersect at the Railway Station Metro called *Vagzlis Moedani*. In 2000 a new station was opened bringing the total number of stations to twenty.

Each station has a small counter where you can buy tokens for 20 tetris per ride.

VISAS AND REGISTRATION

VISAS

Visitors to Tbilisi require a visa. The useful addresses section provides details of the Georgian embassies abroad. You can arrive and collect a visa at the airport but it is more expensive and also involves you spending time at the consular department of the Ministry of Foreign Affairs. You must have a passport that is valid for at least six months after your visit. Visas come in a variety of forms. There are single entry two weeks, one month and three months and multiple entry visas for six months and one year. Prices vary depending upon duration. You will also need a couple of passport photographs and some type of invitation. This can be from a citizen of the country, an organisation based in Georgia or any hotel or travel agent.

If you are travelling on to Azerbaijan or Armenia you will require a visa. Both countries have embassies in Tbilisi, details are in the useful addresses list. Obtaining a visa to travel to Russia overland, i.e., through the North Caucasus is very difficult. Normally you must travel first to Moscow or St. Petersburg.

REGISTRATION

Since late 1999 there has been a requirement for all foreigners to register with the Ministry of Interior. This process came in mainly due to the conflict in Chechenia. Information to date suggests there is nothing sinister going on and the process of registration – automatic if you arrive through Tbilisi Airport – is free.

OTHER PRACTICALITIES

ELECTRICITY

Electricity current is supposed to be 240 volts. The country has been plagued with poor supply for the past ten years and both the quality and quantity of supply are erratic. During the summer months electricity supply at least in Tbilisi is fairly stable but as the weather turns colder so supply worsens. Some parts of the city suffer more than others but there is no discernable pattern from year to year.

Theoretically it is possible to guarantee yourself a twenty-four hour supply if you pay money up front. However one may still be at the whim of the local electricity substation. As much of the power infrastructure is old, cables collapse leaving a street dark for days on end. That said the closer to the centre you live the better the situation is likely to be. It is strongly advised to keep a torch with you and to protect valuable equipment such as computers and televisions with surge protectors. If you are staying for a long period in Tbilisi you may well wish to invest in a generator. One of the best places for purchasing is from the Eliava market in the Didube region. The market is something of a DIY paradise.

EMERGENCIES

If you have a real emergency then the following numbers can be called. The city's fire service can be called on 01, the police on 02. Alternatively call your embassy (see the addresses section) who should be able to help.

ETIQUETTE

There is no particular lore on how to dress or behave. Generally drunkenness is frowned upon. Men tend to dress moderately and unless you want to be stared at shorts should be avoided. Women always dress smartly. When visiting churches and other religious sites dress should be sober. Smoking is forbidden in places of entertainment, on public transport but is allowed everywhere else. Georgia is quite a heavy smoking country and there are no separate sections for smokers in restaurants and bars.

HOLIDAYS

Since independence there has been some confusion over what constitutes a national holiday. The government has tried to introduce new holidays and stop those that are considered Soviet. As Georgia is a predominantly orthodox country religious holidays and festivals follow the Julian calendar. Hence Christmas and Easter are some two weeks after their counterparts in the West. The main holidays when most shops and businesses close are as follows:

New Year – January 1st
Orthodox Christmas – January 7th

Orthodox New Year – January 19th
Mother's Day – March 3rd
Independence Day – May 26th
Mariamoba – August 28th
Svetitskoveloba – October 14th
Tbilisoba – third weekend of October
Giorgoba – November 23rd

LANGUAGE

In most restaurants, hotels, and even the main shops you will probably find that some English is spoken. Since independence English has been challenging Russian as the number two language of Tbilisi. Outside the capital English is much less spoken. Generally if you don't find someone speaking English they may well speak French or German. Just about everyone speaks Russian, except in small pockets in rural areas. The main language of the country is Georgian. It has its own script and is the main language of the South Caucasian or Kartvelian language group. The other languages of the group are Mingrelian spoken in parts of the West of the country, Svan the oldest language of the group still maintained in the mountain region of Svanetia and Laz spoken in some villages in the north east of Turkey. Georgian has thirty-three letters and is characterised by a preponderance of consonant clusters. Most Georgians will tell you that their language is difficult to learn and they are probably right. In most bookshops you can find small phrase books of varying quality. Should you wish to study the language while in Tbilisi the best place to go is The International Centre for Georgian Language Tel. 899 578059 or 899 567144. The suggested reading at the end of this book gives details of various grammars to the language.

LEGAL

Should you require legal services, there are plenty of lawyers' offices in Tbilisi. Many people recommend the GCG Group run by Americans and Georgians. GCG is at 24 Rustaveli Avenue Tel. 936422 Fax. 932752 Email gcglo@caucasus.net. Another firm is Georgian Legal Consulting at 20 Petriashvili Street Tel. 251120 Email GLC@wanex.net. The first consultation with a lawyer is free.

PHOTOGRAPHY

Essentially you can take photographs wherever you want, but military installations should be avoided. Additionally the guards who look after the President can be a little nervous if you take pictures of the President's office and also along the presidential route in the evenings. This is probably because of the two assassination attempts on the President during the nineteen nineties. There are a number of retail outlets that sell film normally for colour prints and they also develop. Slide film and black and white is more difficult to find and should be brought with you.

RENTAL

Longer term visitors may wish to rent an apartment. If you have Georgian colleagues they can probably recommend places through their own networks. A certain element of caution is necessary as sometimes it can be problematic if something goes wrong with the apartment. Better is to rent through an agency as they will sort out contracts and ensure that the landlord knows fully their responsibilities. An apartment in the centre is likely to cost five hundred dollars upwards per month. The following real estate agents are recommended: Center Point 50 Kostava Street *Tel. 920256,* Extra Services 4 Leselidze Street, *Tel. 999418* and Mediators 9/1 Leselidze Street *Tel. 998974.*

When renting it is advisable to ensure that all the utility payments are up to date. There have been some horror stories of people suddenly being faced with huge electricity bills soon after moving in. Additionally there are a number of other payments. There is what is called a communal charge and this should be paid by the landlord. The same is the case for water rates and the rental for the telephone line.

It is quite legal for foreigners to buy property in Georgia and there are some extremely good bargains available, although everything is in need of renovation. You will however need a lawyer and the registration of the property in your name is a tricky procedure as there are at least two places where the property should be registered. Again there have been one or two bad stories or people believing they have bought a property only to find that it has been bought by someone else.

RADIO AND TELEVISION

There are two state run television channels 1 and 2 and one major private channel called Rustavi Two. All broadcast in Georgian. There are also a number of smaller private channels that mainly show Russian dubbed western films. Ayety TV at 6 Kuchishvili Street provides a satellite service and for between $10 and $25 dollars per month (they have different packages and charges depending upon the region of the city), you can receive *CNN, Star World, Star Movies, Euronews, Eurosport, BBC World, Sky News, MTV, ESPN, TV5, Rai Uno, RTL, SAT 1, TVE, National Geographic, Discovery, Fashion TV, Nickleodeon* and a number of Russian channels including *NTV.* Both the BBC World Service Radio and the Voice of America can be received. Local stations tend to be pop orientated but are good to listen to if you want to keep abreast of local Georgian rock and pop.

SPORT

Football is as dominant in Tbilisi as elsewhere. The major team is Dynamo Tbilisi. Both they and the national team play at the National Stadium in Didube. There are four main tennis courts that can be hired. These are at 29 Marjanishvili Street *Tel. 953800* and by the river embankment between the Vorontsov and Baratashvili bridges. There are public courts in Vera and Vake Parks. There is a Bowling Club at 12 Kazbegi Avenue, *Tel. 330350* with six lanes and almost next door at 12a Kazbegi Avenue *Tel. 375693* is a twelve tabled pool club. Those wanting to keep fit may want to use the facilities at the Sheraton Metechi Hotel. The main swimming pool in the city is called Laguna Vera. Prices vary upon the time of day and the day of the week. The address is 34 Kostava Side Street, near the Mtkvari River and down from Heroes Square, *Tel. 998231*. Swimming in Tbilisi Sea, Lisi Lake and Turtle Lake should be avoided as the water quality is variable and cannot be guaranteed.

STREET NAMES

Many of the street names changed when Georgia became independent. The reason was partly to rid the city of Soviet appellations and also to honour new heroes. Unfortunately many locals and particularly taxi drivers do not know the new names. To assist here is a list of the main changes. New names are given first so if you need to ask you can also mention the old name. When enquiring of a street it is also worth giving the region of the city as sometimes the same name is used. For example there are three Sarajishvili Streets, one in the centre and two in the outer suburbs. Also important is the difference between a street (*kucha*) and avenue (*gamziri*). In Georgian street names are placed in the genitive case. Thus using the example of Sarajishvili Street, in Georgian it becomes *Sarajishvilis kucha*, literally the street of Sarajishvili.

New Name	Old Name
Abashidze D.,	Mechnikov St
Abashidze, I., St	Barnov St (after UN)
Abashidze, M. St	Napareuli St
Abesadze St	1st May St
Abo Tbileli St	Kasheni St
Aghmashenebeli Ave.	Plekhanov Avenue
Agladze St	Eliava St
Akhvlediani Rise	Kibalchichi Rise
Akhvlediani St	Perovskaya St
Alexidze St	Rukhadze St
Amagleba St	Davitashvili St
Andronikashvili St	Ulianov St
Antelava St	Iberia St
Anton Catholicos St	Ivanidze St
Areshidze St	Ateni Lane
Asatiani St	Engels St
Bagration St	Toroshelidze St
Beridze St	Tskhakaia St
Botsvadze St	Adleri St
Chanturia St	Jorjiashvili St
Chitaia St	Soviet St
Choloqashvili St	Khuti Decemberi St
Chovelidze St	Belinsky St
Dadiani St	October St
Davitashvili St	Shromi St
Dumas St	Zheliabov St
Eristavi St	Magnitogorsk St
Freedom Square	Lenin Square
Gamrekeli St	Kutuzov St

Gamsakhurdia Ave
Gelovani St
Gorgasali Square
Gudiashvili Square
Gudiashvili St
Gulua St
Gurgenidze St
Iashvili St
Ingorokva St
Iremashvili St
Javakhishvili St
Jerusalem St
Jordania St
Kakabadze Bros St
Kazbegi Avenue
Ketevan t. Martyr Av.
Khandzteli St
Khimshiashvili St
Kikodze St
Kolkheti St
Kostava St
Kurdiani St
Kutateladze St
Laghidze R., St
Leonidze St
Lubovsky St
Managadze St
Manjgaladze St
Margiani St
Meskhia St
Mikatadze St

Mshvidoba Avenue
Luxembourg St
Maiden Square
Alaverdov Square
Ketskoveli St
Didi Kheivni St
Gromov St
Japaridze St
Dzerzhinsky St
Zhgenti St
Elbakidze Rise
Rizhinashvili St
Paraluri St
Leonidze St
Pavlov St
Shaumian St
Myasnikov St
Aliluev St
Makharadze St
Grinevitsky St
Lenin St
Gldani St
Gertzeni St
Lunacharsky St
Kirov St
Aviakimi St
Chodrishvili M., St
Topuridze St
Iashvili St
Gertzeni St
Kiknadze St

Mishveladze St
Ninth April St
Orbeliani Square
Qaraqarashvili St
Radiani St
Rcheulishvili St
Shandize St
Sharashidze St
Shengelia St
Shervashidze St
Skhirtladze St
Skitishvili St
Surguladze St
Svanidze St
Tabukashvili St
Taktakishvili St
Tamarashvili St
Tatishvili Lane
Tatishvili St
Tetelashvili St
Tsinamghvrishvili St
Tsintzadze St
Tsuladze St
26 May Square
Uznadze St
Vekua St
Veshapuri St
Virsaladze St
Zaarbruchen Sq.
Zandukeli St
Zubalashvili Bros St.

Javakhishvili, M St
Chitadze St (end of)
Kolmeurnoba Square
Kakabeti St
Barnov 4th Lane
Sevastopol St
Kalandadze St
Nikoladze St
Gogebashvili 3rd Lane
Vatzeki St
Belostok St
Intskirveli St
Gegechkori St
Gudauri Lane
Dzneladze St
Rigi St
Guramishvili St
Kazbegi Lane
Kazbegi St
Chodrishvili Z., St
Tzetkini St
Saburtalo St
Komkavshiri St
Constitution Square
Camus St
Rusi St
Lelashvili St
Injiniri St
Marx Square
Javakhishvili I., St
Atarbekov St

USEFUL ADDRESSES

EMBASSIES & CONSULATES IN GEORGIA

ARMENIA 4 TETELASHVILI STREET TEL. 959443

AZERBAIJAN 16 MUKHADZE STREET TEL. 234037

CHINA 52 BARNOV STREET TEL. 998011

FRANCE 15 GOGEBASHVILI STREET TEL. 934210

GERMANY 166 AGHMASHENEBELI AVE TEL. 950936

GREECE 5 ARAKISHVILI STREET TEL. 250791

IRAN 16 ZOVRETI STREET TEL. 986990 OR 294502

ISRAEL 61 AGHMASHENEBELI AVENUE TEL. 964457

ITALY RM 334 SHERATON METECHI HOTEL TEL. 946444

NETHERLANDS 27/29 PALIASHVILI ST TEL. 235937

POLAND 19 BROS ZUBALASHVILI STREET TEL. 920398

ROMANIA 7 LVOV STREET TEL. 250098

RUSSIA 90 TSINAMDZGHVRISHVILI ST TEL. 941604

SWEDEN 2 ARAKISHVILI STREET TEL. 292676

TURKEY 61 AGHMASHENEBELI AVENUE TEL. 952014

UKRAINE 75 ONIASHVILI STREET TEL. 989362

UNITED KINGDOM SHERATON METECHI HOTEL TEL. 998447

UNITED STATES OF AMERICA 25 ATONELI STREET TEL. 989968

GEORGIAN EMBASSIES ABROAD

ARMENIA 42 ARAMIS STREET, EREVAN. TEL. 374 2 585511 FAX. 374 2 564183

AUSTRIA MAROKKANERGASSE 16, A1130 VIENNA. TEL. 43 1 710 3611 FAX. 43 1 7103610

AZERBAIJAN HOTEL AZERBAIJAN 13/F, 1 AZADLIGI AVE, BAKU TEL. 994 12 981779 FAX. 994 12 989440

BELGIUM 15 RUE VERGOTE, 1030 BRUSSELS TEL. 32 2 732 8550 FAX. 32 2 732 8547

FRANCE 104 RAYMOND POINCARÉ AVENUE, 75116 PARIS TEL. 33 1 4502 1616 FAX. 33 1 4502 1601

GERMANY 6 AM KURPARK, BONN 53177. TEL. 49 228 9575112 FAX. 49 228 9575120

GREECE 24 AGIOU DIMITRIOU STREET, PALEO PSIHIO, 15452 ATHENS TEL. 30 1 671 6737 FAX. 30 1 671 6722

IRAN 36 MOTTAGHIAN STREET, FAMANIEH, TEHRAN. TEL. 98 21 229 5135 FAX. 98 21 229 5136

ISRAEL 74/5 HEI BE 'IYAR KIKAR, HAMEDINA, TEL AVIV 62198 TEL. 972 3 604 3232 FAX. 972 3 602 1542

ITALY 20 PIAZZA DI SPAGNA, PLAZZA PIERRET, 00187 ROME TEL. 39 6 69941972 FAX. 39 6 69941942

RUSSIA 6 MALII RZHESKII, MOSCOW 121069. TEL. 7 095 290 6902 FAX. 7 095 291 4129

SWITZERLAND 1 RUE RICHARD WAGNER, 1202 GENEVA. TEL. 41 22 9191010 FAX. 41 22 733 9033

TURKEY 15 ABDULLAH CEVDET SOK, GNKAYA, ANKARA. TEL. 90 312 4426508 FAX. 90 312 4426510

UNITED KINGDOM 3 HORNTON PLACE, LONDON W8 4LZ TEL. 44 171 937 8233 FAX. 44 171 938 4108

UNITED STATES OF AMERICA 1511 NEW HAMPSHIRE AVE. N. W. SUITE 300, WASHINGTON D.C. 20009. TEL. 1 202 393-5959 FAX. 1 202 393 4537

GEORGIAN GOVERNMENT

PRESIDENTIAL PRESS OFFICE 7 INGOROKVA ST TEL. 999653

AGRICULTURE 41 KOSTAVA STREET TEL. 990272

COMMUNICATIONS & TRANSPORT 12 RUSTAVELI AVENUE TEL. 999528

CULTURE 37 RUSTAVELI AVENUE TEL. 932255

DEFENCE 2 UNIVERSITY STREET TEL. 303163

ECONOMY, IND. & TRADE 12 CHANTURIA ST. TEL. 982743

EDUCATION 52 UZNADZE STREET TEL. 958886

ENVIRONMENT 68A KOSTAVA STREET TEL. 230664

FINANCE 70 IRAKLI ABASHIDZE STREET TEL. 226805

FOREIGN AFFAIRS 4 CHITADZE STREET TEL. 989377

FUEL & ENERGY 10 LERMONTOV ST. TEL. 996098

HEALTH 30 GAMSAKHURDIA AVENUE TEL. 221235

INTERIOR 10 GULUA STREET TEL. 996296

JUSTICE 30 RUSTAVELI AVENUE TEL. 934929

REFUGEES 28 RUSTAVELI AVENUE TEL. 941611

SECURITY 4 NINTH APRIL STREET TEL. 922315

STATE PROPERTY 64 CHAVCHAVADZE AVE. TEL. 294875

INTERNATIONAL ORGANISATIONS

EUROPEAN COMMISSION DELEGATION, 38 NINO CHKHEIDZE STREET TEL. 943763

EUROPEAN BANK FOR RECONSTRUCTION AND DEVELOPMENT, 38 NINO CHKHEIDZE STREET TEL. 920512

INT. COMMITTEE OF THE RED CROSS, 4 KEDIA STREET TEL. 935511

INT FEDERATION OF RED CROSS AND RED CRESCENT SOCIETIES, 7 ANTON CATHOLICOS STREET TEL. 951404

INTERNATIONAL MONETARY FUND, ROOM 230, 7 INGOROKVA STREET TEL. 936601

INTERNATIONAL ORGANISATION FOR MIGRATION, 41 GOGEBASHVILI STREET TEL. 293894

ORGANISATION FOR SECURITY AND COOPERATION IN EUROPE, DACHA 5, KRTSANISI RESIDENCE TEL. 988205

UNITED NATIONS, 9 ERISTAVI STREET TEL. 998558

UN HIGH COMMISSIONER FOR REFUGEES 2A KAZBEGI AVENUE TEL. 250080

WORLD FOOD PROGRAMME 39A CHAVCHAVADZE AVENUE TEL. 253667

WORLD BANK 18A CHONKADZE STREET TEL. 942848

TRAVEL

AIRZENA, 5 MELIKISHVILI STREET TEL. 294053

AUSTRIAN AIRLINES 20 TELAVI STREET TEL. 778214

BRITISH AIRWAYS SHERATON METECHI HOTEL TEL. 940719/20

SWISS AIR SHERATON METECHI HOTEL TEL. 943825/26

TURKISH AIRLINES 147 AGHMASHENEBELI AVE. TEL. 959022

CENTRAL RAILWAY STATION, 2 STATION SQUARE TEL. 994760

TBILISI JUNCTION STATION, 2 MOSCOW AVENUE TEL. 716733, 716030

DIDUBE BUS STATION, 4 KARALETI STREET TEL. 344140

ORTACHALA BUS STATION, 2 GULUA STREET TEL. 723433

CAUCASUS TRAVEL , 5-7 SHAVTELI STREET TEL. 987400

EXTRA SERVICES GEORGIAN TOUR LINES, 4 LESELIDZE STREET TEL. 999418

GEORGICA TRAVEL, 13 SHANIDZE STREET TEL. 227595

LEVON TRAVEL, 20 CHAVCHAVADZE AVE TEL. 250010

SAK TOUR, 32 BARNOV STREET TEL. 982966

THOMAS COOK, 19 MARJANISHVILI ST TEL. 960139

SUGGESTED READING

TBILISI
DJANBERIDZE, N. & MATCHABELI, K. *Tbilisi Mzheta Tbilisi Mtskheta.* Moscow: *Iskusstvo,* 1981. *In Russian.*

GERSAMIYA, TAMAZ *Dzveli Tbilisi Old Tbilisi.* Tbilisi: *Sabchota Sakartvelo,* 1984. *In Georgian, Russian and English.*

KHUTSISHVILI, GEORGY *Tbilisi a guide.* Moscow: *Planeta Publishers,* 1989.

KVIRKVELIYA, TENGIZ *Staruy Tbilisi.* Tbilisi: *Sabchota Sakartvelo,* 1985. *In Russian.*

KVIRKVELIYA, TENGIZ *Po ulitsam i pereulkam starogo Tbilisi.* Tbilisi: *Sabchota Sakartvelo,* 1989. *In Russian.*

SUMBADZE, L. *The Georgian Museum of National Architecture and Ethnography in the Open Air.* Tbilisi: *Sabchota Sakartvelo,* 1978.

TBILISIS ISTORIA TOM 1. Tbilisi: *Metsniereba,* 1990. *In Georgian.*

TSITSISHVILI, IRAKLI *Tbilisi Architectural Landmarks and Art Museums.* Leningrad: *Aurora Art Publishers,* 1985.

INTRODUCTION AND TRAVEL
BARNARD, ANDREW *The Smart Guide to Georgia.* Tbilisi: *Smart Ltd.,* 1999.

BITOV, ANDREI *A Captive of the Caucasus.* London: *Weidenfeld & Nicolson,* 1992.

BURFORD, TIM *Georgia, the Bradt Travel Guide.* Chalfont St. Peter, Bucks: *Bradt,* 1999.

DUMAS, ALEXANDER *Adventures in Caucasia.* London: *Chilton Books,* 1962.

ELLIOT, MARK *Azerbaijan with Georgia.* Hindhead, Surrey: *Trailblazer Publications,* 1999.

FARSON, NEGLEY *Caucasian Journey.* Harmondsworth: *Penguin,* 1988.

GACHECHILADZE REVAZ *The New Georgia.* London: *UCL Press,* 1995.

LANG, DAVID *The Georgians.* London: *Thames and Hudson,* 1966.

MACLEAN, FITZROY *To Caucasus, the end of all the earth: an illustrated companion to the Caucasus and Transcaucasia.* London: *Jonathan Cape,* 1976.

MARSDEN, PHILIP *The Spirit Wrestlers.* London: *Harper Collins,* 1998.

NASMYTH, PETER *Georgia: A Rebel in the Caucasus.* London: *Cassell,* 1992.

NASMYTH, PETER *Georgia in the Mountains of Poetry.* Richmond, Surrey: *Curzon Press,* 1998. In paperback 2000.

PEREIRA, MICHAEL *Across the Caucasus.* London: *Geoffry Bless,* 1973.

ROSEN, ROGER *Georgia, a Sovereign Country of the Caucasus.* Hong Kong: *Odyssey Publications,* 1999.

RUSSELL, MARY *Please Don't Call it Soviet Georgia*. London: *Serpent's Tail*, 1991.

THUBRON, COLIN *Among the Russians*. London: *William Heinemann*, 1983.

WARDROP, OLIVER *The Kingdom of Georgia*. London: *Sampson Low Marston, Searle & Rivington*, 1888. (reprinted 1976).

WILSON, NEIL, POTTER BETH, ROWSON DAVID & JAPARIDZE KETI *Georgia, Armenia & Azerbaijan*. Melbourne: *Lonely Planet*, 2000.

HISTORY
ALLEN, W.E.D. *A History of the Georgian People*. London: *Kegan Paul*, 1932. (Reprinted Barnes & Noble, 1971.)

ALLEN, W.E.D. & MURATOV, P. *Caucasian Battlefields*. Cambridge: *Cambridge University Press*, 1953.

ARBEL, RACHEL & MAGAL, LILY *In the Land of the Golden Fleece: The Jews of Georgia; History and Culture*. Tel Aviv: *Ministry of Defence Publishing House*, 1992.

ASCHERSON, NEAL *The Black Sea*. London: *Jonathan Cape*, 1995.

BADDELEY, JOHN F. *The Russian Conquest of the Caucasus*. Richmond, Surrey: *Curzon Press*, 1997.

BRAUND, DAVID *Georgia in Antiquity: a history of Colchis and Transcaucasian Iberia*. Oxford: *Clarendon Press*, 1994.

BURNEY, CHARLES & LANG, DAVID *The Peoples of the Hills*. London: *Weidenfeld & Nicolson*, 1971.

CHARACHIDZE, GEORGES *Introduction à l'étude de la féodalite géorgienne*. Paris: 1971.

LANG, DAVID *A Modern History of Georgia*. London: *Weidenfeld & Nicolson*, 1962.

LANG, DAVID *The Last Years of the Georgian Monarchy, 1658-1832*. New York: *Columbia University Press*, 1957.

MACLEAN, FITZROY *Eastern Approaches*. London: *Jonathan Cape*, 1949.

MINORSKY, VLADIMIR *Studies in Caucasian History*. London: *Cambridge Oriental Series*, 1953.

RHINELANDER, L.H. *The Incorporation of the Caucasus into the Russian Empire: The case of Georgia*. New York: *Columbia University Press*, 1972.

SALIA, KALISTRAT *Histoire de la nation géorgienne*. Paris: *Éd. Nino Salia*, 1980.

SUNY, RONALD *The Making of the Georgian Nation*. 2nd ed. Bloomington: *Indiana University Press*, 1994.

SUNY, RONALD (ed.) *Transcaucasia, Nationalism and Social Change*. Ann Arbor: *Michigan Slavic Publications*, 1983.

TOUMANOFF, CYRIL *Manuel de généalogie et de chronologie pour l'histoire de la Caucasie Chrétienne*. Rome: *Edizioni Aquila*, 1976.

147

TOUMANOFF, CYRIL *Studies in Christian Caucasian History*. Washington D.C.: *Georgetown University Press*, 1963.

VIVIAN, KATHERINE (trans.) *The Georgian Chronicle, the period of Giorgi Lasha*. Amsterdam: *Adolf M. Hakkart*, 1991.

ECONOMICS AND POLITICS
AVALOV, ZURAB *The Independence of Georgia in International Politics, 1918-1921*. London: *Headley Brothers*, 1940.

AVES, JONATHAN *Georgia: From Chaos to Stability*. London: *Chatham House*, 1995.

BROOK, STEPHEN *The Claws of the Crab*. London: *Picador*, 1992.

CHERVONNAYA SVETLANA *Conflict in the Caucasus*. Glastonbury: *Gothic Image Publications*, 1994.

ECONOMIST INTELLIGENCE UNIT *Georgia & Armenia - Country Reports*. London: *EIU*, 2000-.

GEORGIAN ECONOMIC TRENDS Tbilisi: *Georgian Economic Trends*, 1995-

MCGIFFERT EKEDAHL, CAROLYN & GOODMAN, MELVIN A. *The Wars of Eduard Shevardnadze*. London: *Hurst & Company*, 1997.

GOLDENBERG, SUZANNE *The Pride of Small Nations*. London: *Zed Press*, 1994.

JONES, STEPHEN *Georgian Social Democracy in Opposition and Power*. London: *University of London*, 1984.

KAZEMZADEH, FIRUZ *The Struggle for Transcaucasia, 1918-1921*. New York: *Philosophical Library*, 1951.

SHEVARDNADZE, EDUARD *The Future Belongs to Freedom*. New York: *Sinclair Stevenson*, 1991.

WRIGHT, JOHN F.R., GOLDENBERG, SUZANNE AND SCHOFIELD, RICHARD (eds.) *Transcaucasian Boundaries*. London: *UCL Press*, 1996.

ART AND ARCHITECTURE
BULIA, MARINA & JANJALIA, MZIA *Mtskheta*. Tbilisi: *Betania*, 2000.

EASTMOND, ANTHONY *Royal Imagery in Medieval Georgia*. University Park, PA: *Pennsylvania University Press*, 1998.

MEPISASHVILI, RUSUDAN AND TSINTSADZE, VAKHTANG *The Arts of Ancient Georgia*. New York: *Thames and Hudson*, 1979.

SOLTES, ORI Z. National Treasures of Georgia. London: *Philip Wilson Publishers Ltd.*, 1999.

REISSNER, ILMA *La Géorgie, Histoire, art, culture*. Turnhout: *Brepols*, 1990.

VELMANS, TANIA *L'arte della Georgia: affreschi e architetture*. Milan: *Jaca Books*, 1996.

CUISINE
GOLDSTEIN, DARRA *The Georgian Feast*. New York: *Harper & Collins*, 1993.

MARGVELASHVILI, JULIANNE *The Classic Cuisine of Soviet Georgia*. New York: *Prentice Hall Press*, 1991.

HOLISKY, DEE ANN *The Rules of the Supra or How to Drink in Georgian*. JOURNAL FOR THE STUDY OF CAUCASIA, VOL 1, NO.1.

LANGUAGE
ARONSON, HOWARD *Georgian: a reading grammar, corrected edition*. Columbus, Ohio: *Slavica Publishers*, 1990.

AWDE, NICHOLAS AND KHITARISHVILI, THEA. *Georgian-English English-Georgian dictionary and phrasebook*. Richmond, Surrey: *Curzon Press*, 1997.

CATFORD, J.C. *Mountains of tongues: the languages of the Caucasus*. ANNUAL REVIEW OF ANTHROPOLOGY, VOL. 6, 1977.

HEWITT, GEORGE *Georgian: a learner's grammar*. London: *Routledge*, 1996.

HEWITT, GEORGE *Georgian: a structural reference grammar*. Amsterdam: *John Benjamins*, 1996.

LITERATURE
BLANCH, LESLEY *The Sabres of Paradise*. London: *John Murray*, 1960.

LAYTON SUSAN *Russian literature and empire: conquest of the Caucasus from Pushkin to Tolstoy*. New York: *Cambridge University Press*, 1994.

LERMONTOV, MIKHAIL *A Hero of Our Time*. Harmondsworth: *Penguin*, 1977.

PASTERNAK, BORIS *Letters to Georgian Friends*. London: *Secker and Warburg*, 1968.

PUSHKIN, ALEXANDRE *A journey to Erzrum*. Glastonbury: *Ardis Publishers*, 1974.

RAYFIELD, DONALD *The Literature of Georgia*. Richmond, Surrey: *Curzon Press*, 1998.

RUSTAVELI, SHOTA *The Man in the Panther's Skin*. trans. Marjory Wardrop. London: *Royal Asiatic Society*, 1912.

RUSTAVELI, SHOTA *The Knight in the Panther's Skin*. trans. R.H. Stevenson. New York: *State University of New York Press*, 1977.

SAID, KURBAN *Ali and Nino*. London: *Robin Clark Ltd.*, 1990.

URUSHADZE, VENERA *Anthology of Georgian Poetry*. Tbilisi: *State Publishing House*, 1958.

RELIGION
ALFEYEVA, VALERIA *Pilgrimage to Dzhvari: A Woman's Journey of Spiritual Awakening*. New York: *Bell Tower Press*, 1995.

MGALOBLISHVILI, TAMILA (ed.) *Ancient Christianity in the Caucasus*. Richmond, Surrey: *Curzon Press*, 1998.

LANG, DAVID *Lives and legends of the Georgian saints*. London: *Allen & Unwin*, 1956.